D1188380

MORTAL FIRE

"Man is no starre, but a quick coal
Of mortall fire . . ."
George Herbert

PETER DALE

MORTAL FIRE

OHIO UNIVERSITY PRESS
ATHENS, OHIO

ACKNOWLEDGEMENTS: An earlier version of *Mortal Fire* was first published by Macmillan (London) in 1970. This version has been expanded with poems from my first book *The Storms*, published by Macmillan (London) in 1968. My thanks are also due to Agenda Editions (London) for allowing me to reprint translations from my *Seasons of Cankam* (1974).

The poem *Gift of Words* first appeared in *The Young British Poets*, edited by Jeremy Robson, published by Chatto & Windus and Corgi Books (London) 1971. Others have appeared in my pamphlet *Interims*, published by The Hippopotamus Press (Sutton, Surrey) 1975.

Versions of poems from *The Going* have appeared in the following periodicals: *Agenda; Meridian; The New Statesman; Poetry Nation; The Review; The Southern Review; Stand; The Times Literary Supplement* and *Tribune*.

Kind permission has also been granted by St. Martin's Press (New York) and Macmillan (London) to reprint "Epitaph of Villon."

ISBN 0-8214-0185-8 Cloth
ISBN 0-8214-0187-4 Paper
Library of Congress Catalog No. LC 74-29409
Printed in the United States of America by The Watkins Printing Co.
Designed by Harold M. Stevens

DEDICATION To P.

Your presence, love,
like the underlight
of trees within a wood,
that quiet pleasure
I could always predict,
often request.

But to tell you
somehow share
this pleasure in writing,
always unbidden,
seldom predicted,
and solitary.

This you request of me
and I in return
promise to share
these ten years past
yet find no words,
none like your presence.

MORTAL FIRE

FRAGMENTS

UNADDRESSED LETTER

I had no need to come to your funeral.
I heard the news only by telegraph.
The shock I felt was distant and unreal.
Nor was there with me one so aged with grief
to need an escort to this open grave.
A letter could have made my peace instead.
I had no need to come, yet there I stood.

Neighbours, as I suspected, came to the grave
to watch the son they backed at lunch for signs
of tears, the sobbing stoop of hidden grief.
I knew. Though I must have left home long since.
Keith's tears moved me no more than anyone's.
I watched them watch. But when ropes ran to inter
you there I saw a brown leaf give under a tear.

Sheep on the hills like huge maggots. 'God shall wipe
away all tears from their eyes
and there shall be no more death to weep,
neither shall there be any pain or disease . . .'
Something like that as mud sucked at my shoes.
I watched ashamed for fear your friends might smell
your sinking flesh that stank like an animal. . . .

Now it is autumn and rain. Big drops you can trace.
I notice how one drop's enough to tear
an amber leaf out of the brittle trees.
I suppose much the same happened last year,
but it's now I notice, watching a caricature
of your face talking to myself as I stare
out of the window where the puddles stir.

And there are other words I would have had
for you. I should have said how I left home
because I feared those wounds your meekness hid
might breed in me. If I used an idiom
of yours I'd break off. I watched my face become
your likeness. My temper fought your reticence
from me. I left to think you happier since.

I could only say this now you're dead. I know
it cannot wound you secretly. I'm sorry.
Perhaps those letters would have had my new
address if I'd said all this at home in Surrey.
But you are dead now and it isn't necessary.
You could have posted them. Your wrinkles soon
will ride my features. And in this silence I'm your son.

The window reflects the galleon of fire still
yards off in the dark, some useless knick-knack.
Rain drips regularly from the loose tile.
A wren ruffles the feathers round its neck,
sheltering in the gutter from the muffled knocks
of continual rain. Time to draw the blinds.
The galleon vanishes. A leaf zigzags as it lands.

THE FRAGMENTS

My life must be Christ's broken bread,
My love His outpoured wine,
A cup o'erfilled, a table spread
Beneath his name and sign,
That other souls refreshed and fed
May share His life through mine . . .

Now they've returned by post the book of hymns
you gave me. It stands narrow among mine,
goldbacked and ribbed like bamboo cane,
cleaner than the rest. You and your horn-rims
weren't given to read a line.
This music now and again
comes by me. Sometimes the words fill my head;
they speak with my desires but not your hope.
I try to change them for lines you haven't read—
with books you couldn't cope.

Grief fills the room up of my absent son . . .

They bring back evenings of study in my room.
Chords rolled from the organ keys you spanned,
the whole house empty. You couldn't read a bar.
Only the tune and an octave's occasional boom.
Sometimes I couldn't stand
those wrong notes. They'd jar
your loneliness against me. I'd come downstairs
and make your supper and we would sit and eat
in silence separated by your stumbling airs
and our eyes would not meet.

He talks to me who never had a son . . .

And once, the cup slipping, I made some stains
upon the cloth. The handle wasn't there,
I joked, and dropped the names of idealists.
At once your face spidered with broken veins.
I still remember that stare,
those wildly beating fists.
You thought an upset milkjug proved your case.
We sat angrily mute, pretending neat
cocoa was good. You muttered some routine grace
but I'd begun to eat.

Take ye eat for this is my body . . .

Yet every meal was Eucharist for you
and your religion. I used to say you ate
far too much fat but you would only hedge.
Though more than I could ever warn you knew
and scarcely could forget
words that had such edge.
You knew there was no hope of cure or ease
to come, not even from a surgeon's knife,
but never spoke a word of this disease
to anyone in your life.

He that would gain his life shall lose it . . .

I chanced to tread on a stagbeetle on the walk
from the house. It crunched like wickerwork.
But when you, father, fell and came to die
no detonation wrecked the streets that day.
A great matter went out of the universe
and nothing shook beneath its radiant force.
It should have knocked a world to stellar dust
but only a day or two were my hands dazed.
Yet now I mind my step in a distant town
as though a mine were buried at each turn.

Erratic clack of typing rackets and cracks
throughout my room. Two-fingered my hands,
like feelered insects, pick at the crowded keys.
The table echoes the clacks.
A miner trapped by land-
slide, tapping on his knees
to contact rescue. But you're the buried one.
I know the ways between us, the walls and loosestrife,
letters unposted, journals in unison.
I'm the resurrection and the life.

Blessed are the meek. The missioners all came
to the graveside to pay you their respects.
You would have been encouraged by the crowd.
No other occasion you could ever name
drew such numbers of your sect.
I must say they did you proud.
Of course, you realize it was mid-week
and they must work to eat. And who'd suggest
they knew no christian aid that you might seek
from them that day of rest?

The cortege stopped.
And drop-jowl, the funerealist,
steadied my arm as I stepped
out of his Rolls at last.
I shrugged myself free,
my hands clenching:
the death of a father
is not debilitating.

Few ever came to help you speak or sell
your tracts and gospels in the village square
to neighbours queued for buses to a town
of cinemas and more than one hotel.
I saw your gesture tear
archaic period and noun
across the dusk, but walked with friends to the pub,
pretending not to see your stand or the stare
of neighbours as they noticed one more snub.
And he could do no miracle there.

'"Being in the form of God,
he thought it not robbery
to be equal with God
but made himself of no reputation
and took upon him the form of a servant
and was brought to the likeness of man . . ."'
Your odd, tobyjug figure shook:
'"and fashioned as a man
he humbled himself
and became obedient unto death,
even the death of the cross.
Wherefore God hath given him a name . . ."'
And then you gasped for breath.

Strawlight stuffing poked from the bare light.
Crumpets of foam topped each icicled glass.
You entered the bar to sell your magazines
around the mellow. When they claimed their right
to hymns from bible-class,
recalling childhood scenes,
I watched your hands fumble out some harmony.
You offered me your box. Coins would chink
in silence and you whisper: '"He that hath no money
come ye to the waters and drink."'

And now I watch my hands fumble the keys,
my type no better than your tunes—those weak,
incurving little-fingers, the family trait,
never to make the furthest stretch with ease.
All you have left: a unique
inheritance I hate.
Downstairs the strumming guts of guitars
and gramophones replace your wheezing tunes.
I watch acquaintances head for various bars.
The docile busqueue moons.

6,000,000 Guinness drunk every day

The type lies regular across the sheet
that takes no record of the typing speed.
Your weakness seemed beatitude when read
into double columns and neat
print of your bible creed.
But under another head
the medical book asserts:
    "Angina attacks a given type of person,
    people pressed too much by nervous wor-
    ry to relax. The only cure is rest."

Come unto me all ye that labour . . .

You daren't sit still as we'd have made you sit
if you had mentioned this. Silence thinned
to screaming in your ears. Keith said to me
that working in your room you had a fit
of coughing, complained of wind
and asked for a cup of tea.
He found you sprawling dead against the wall,
the cup shattered.
                    And I recalled our rows
when you spilt tea in your rush to the mission-hall
from your delapidated house.

    I never saw the mourners when I worked
    in hospitals. They were an embarrassment.
    I busied myself with other things—jerked
    the cover straight or scrutinized the dead.
    Without shock then I watched the others bent
    around your blood-bulging, veinshot head.
    Tearless, I saw Keith as though again
    he stumbled with your body as the stair
    blurred into tears, his hands moist with strain.
    And he, sensing my look, straightened his back.

Dear dust, you never knew how great your hurt.
Spending your time to comfort other folk
in pain, yours had no power to make you scream.
Then once it stopped you short, drenching your shirt
with sweat, making you choke—
Nothing . . . or so it would seem
besides accounts you heard them give of pain.
Feverish still, but restless, you rose from bed
to nurse your wife. Your heart failed under the strain.
The wounds of others struck you dead.

I watch them stand solemnly in that queue,
loaded with goods, without grimace or smile.
You'd handle them with tracts and pious books.
You always made out something you could do.
And now I watch them file
to see some film that looks
once more into the concentration camps.
This, how their victims queued, some accounts said.
Night fall. My face projects in the glow of the lamps.
They move about my head.

6,000,000 . . .

ROOTED IN EARTH

RADIUM THERAPY

Deflated of flesh,
like axehafts,
the shinbones poke from rumpled bedding.

I hurry past
to avoid the radiation field.
The sweat and stench would make one retch.

But turn
to put the blankets straight.
And, leaning through the field,
I warm myself a little in my haste.

THE VISITORS

They know no more than I would how to stand
with flowers, and being men, sheepishly clutch
them, elbows stiffly bent,
as though a touch
of clothes or hand
would wither up the bloom and kill the scent.
They do not know the odd resilience of flowers.
They wait for wife's or child's visiting hours.

Shot on jets of green the tulips zoom
and weigh their stems across the corridors,
heavy and symmetric as eggs.
The visitors
need so much room
the trolleys brush the flowers or knock their legs.
They hinder the stretcher bearing one whose life
hangs in the balance. Someone else's wife.

Then for a nurse they thin to single file
and let her through to supper as though she rushed
to tend an injury.
Awkward and hushed,
they try a smile
then shift and fidget, stood without dignity
at the beck and call of junior nurse or maid,
shielding their flowers, helpless, almost afraid.

PATIENT

He holds his hand out like a sunflower drooping,
palm foremost on stalky wrist, the fingers
undone in dead petals hooking backward.

But this is no paper flower held waiting
in charity upon the street corners
to pass by with twopence or blank eyes lowered.

The pain he's in. It is death thrusting
his hand out. I've nothing to give that matters—
there's little powerful enough if offered.

How can I go and explain to him saying
I'm not qualified to administer the painkillers?
The words are long beside the need unanswered.

PASSING THE GATES

The fountain at the entrance in the square
with its thin dribble drizzling to the pool
that I always hear when going anywhere
today surprises me with silence, its drool
berged on the stone lit green by sun and slime.
Quiet recalls old Tom, the gateman, who'll
be thinking ice broke his thigh about this time.

Most doctors, picking up their mail, implied
he'd always need a stick. Yet summer came
and he was walking with his usual stride.
Fall came, and surgeons, checking all the same,
thought colostomy urgent. . . . Trees gawked bare
and somehow he was once more walking lame
when he returned to the fountain-drizzled square.

The impossible Pan, birdshot and tumbledown,
like an armless Deposition, drips once more
into my ears as I walk toward the town.
Tap drips loudening to a roar
in restless sleep. I haven't visited
Old Tom. And now I stride on past the door
again, being afraid he might be dead.

EMERGENCY GASTRECTOMY

Sent for this case, I found an executive
too overweight for one to lift alone.

I thought, awaiting help with eighteen stone,
you'll weigh less to bring back if you live.

But later when I took him back to bed
his swag of flesh was harder still to lift.

There were blood-drip, saline and flush to shift,
three bottles to be kept above the head.

Sweating and winded, we dumped the slipping load.
I freed my arms—my hands were covered in blood.

JUST VISITING

I walk awkwardly between the beds in row
trying to avoid the gauntlet of levelled eyes
like beggars that ask and envy me the ease
with which I take this tailored body through.

And you are one of these faces. At first
unseen, then recognized right down the ward.
Slight twitch of greeting because I would
n't like to wear that far a smile held fast.

You whine how much your cut hurts. You tell
me nurses forced you up to pack their wads
for sterilizing, made you decorate the ward's
long walls with flowers. And you quite ill.

I'm supposed to be horrified, to sympathize.
Yet nurses have to get the dressings done,
nightly have boys to lay and drinks to down
like you to make their leaving home worth this.

Sister's periods, the old and wrinkled faces
pursed on nerve-strings to the clenched lips,
hours of obedience enough to bring collapse
on hangover, and then, cleaning up faeces.

And some of them have indolent golden hair.
Over there a woman is dying, the line
of used laughter hung in bands on the lean
bones. And what you say I cannot hear.

I shudder. If your eyes started to glaze
I should listen now, although it could not lead
again to lively talk, drinks, light to slide
about your belly like brandy in a glass.

Such compassion couldn't turn a grey hair
auburn, nor startle your brows. But you will live again
and the living need a little love to go on.
You can speak now. I am here.

ELEGY

People waiting at the bus-stop.
Oscillographs of light on the road.
Nothing to show a bus will draw up.

Put a corpse in the morgue and saw them
patiently waiting. Nine in the morgue.
And one in bedsocks. The buses seldom

come. We laughed. A phone-message
waiting back at the porters' lodge:
ward nine: another due for cartage.

People waiting at the bus-stop.
Oscillographs of light on the road.
Nothing to show a bus will turn up.

Bone holds erect the body
but dead flesh bears the full weight
of its skeleton. All corpses are skinny.

We lift you, feel earth drawing
bone down, gouging through the flesh.
Some are more accommodating

dead. But If I remember rightly
not you. We take you in an embrace
that would move any woman, my lovely.

But this is the last warmth we, or
any, shall have of you. And it occurs
to me first. We close the trolley cover.

So I suppose it's something like love this
taking you gently aside, assuming
you flamed with thighs before your illness.

And I do appreciate this, though
it leaves no room for sentimentality.
This corpse is dead to my sorrow.

What should I have known, I wonder,
to qualify. As with you, an autumn
burned through her hair styled for anger.

And walking through those woods last winter
I might have said: 'Stop, your walk
disturbs the stars.' And paused beside her.

Maybe she dressed your style at leisure
in rooms of such disorder nothing
could be out of place around her.

None of this. Like you, she was never
still, I suppose, woman so live
that the dead have been dead for ever.

People waiting at the bus-stop.
Oscillographs of light on the road.
No bus is likely to show up.

I join the queue.

HAVING NO ALTERNATIVE

'The sun shone, having no alternative, on the nothing new . . .'
Beckett *Murphy*

MEETING

I would hardly have remembered your face
but then you used that strange word *wayzgoose*
and it didn't seem out of place
in your chinese-miniaturist choice of words.
Heard once it stayed in mind as your monogram,
recalled your Irish voice.

Then you left town
without a word
and I had this
as a memory of you,
this odd, misleading sound
for your medieval feasts of beer.

Returned unexpectedly after a year
you discover someone relishing a word
you thought your own,
and in sheer delight now
you make him one to drink with here
but never bring to mind
how oddly this introduction was done.

Your dragonfly mind
hovered where seconds flower.

QUICK ONE

Your local—for a day or two.

'The road winds to the crack of doom
Across the peaks and quagmire.
And when you turn the last long bend
There's one more left to dog-tire.'

'The road stops when I want to stop.
The road lies down with me, flat.
The road will always reach the top
Of any hill I see, Pat.'

'Now, Murphy, don't you know the way?
The road runs to the Jailhouse
And by the church and round the dole
And never past an Alehouse.'

You always went for a song.

'No, Patrick, sure the road I know
Like the head o' my jar of guzzle
It links the stars up in its way
Like a children's dotty puzzle.'

'Now where's your sense o' direction gone?
The clouds on rails like carriages
Run on this road and rattle rain
And then comes hail in barrages.'

‘No, Patrick, where’s your wanderlust?
    The clouds, ’tis true, are carriages.
But sure they pour the rain in pints
    And this road stops at Claridges.’

‘Now where’s your sense o’ direction gone?
    You’ve passed the time of day by
And pass it by again tonight.
    When will we find a lay-by?’

‘I’ve one direction more to lose
    And when I’ve lost it, Patrick,
I’ll spin a coin and turn a bend
    Because I’ll have the hat-trick.’

‘The road goes through the Temperance Straits
    And fills me boots with water;
And then it passes through the town
    And will not stop for porter.’

Two pints of bitter, please.
And knock the handles off!

‘But if it fills your boots too full
    The holes right through the uppers
Will let the water out again
    Before it fills your scuppers.’

‘The road winds to the crack of doom
    Across the peaks and quagmire.
And when you round the last lone bend
    You never find a log-fire.’

Let's go before they sing
The National Anthem.

'The road winds to the crack of doom
And when I've gone the distance
I'll take my pick and mend the crack
And save your boots from mischance.'

Stage Irish.
England your stage, Murphy.

THE RUNAWAY

He came back here after food, shelter, the day.
And I welcomed him delighted as he stood.
Here was no layabout, addict or crook.
This was Murphy, my old distracted stray,
bringing for luggage as usual a book
of Yeats and the grey duffel with the hood.

So we fixed a meal and as usual he split
the thick Darjeeling and I threw him most
of the bedding, remembering he slept cold.
And then I left him sprawling under the quilt
on the sofa, flicking through Yeats as of old.
And I dashed out to catch the late post.

When I returned he was soundly asleep
as if nothing had happened to make him quit.
He'd made my bed, too, though I had slept
weeks without worry or fear, I took the heap
of bedding he'd returned, but as I crept
to put it back he woke screaming as if hit.

THE COAT

My room again, tidy and chill at dusk
after a week away: the furniture
uncluttered, ash-trays clean. But on the chair
the coat you borrowed, books back on the desk.

I recall the days your nervy hands would make
the ash-trays overflow with dog-ends, curled
yellow like dead wasps. But today you called
and never waited long enough to smoke.

I try on the coat. It seems unlike you, queer
there's nothing to return in any pocket.
Hundreds of dead matches. An empty packet.
You smoke so much while waiting anywhere.

Crossing to put the books away, I stop.
My body shudders.
The feel of your shoulders
left in the coat has given me your stoop.

I couldn't wear it in the town for folk
would recognize the style and so assume
we know each other. There's nothing but some
distance between us now.
                                        And which fork
you took along St Giles I do not know.

COURTESY VISIT

In the small hours—
the din of voices in my ears—
you storm the stairs.

You reach my room for sanctuary
and drum upon the door,
then ram.

Almost in sleep-walk I open up.
You slump in,
weak, scarcely awake.

I turn the lock against them,
make Darjeeling,
black as you like it.

Cheeks veined with spider mauves,
your eyes blink slowly like fish mouths.
No muscle moves.

You've been on the drugs again.

THE TERMS

If I should suddenly hear that you were ill,
arrested or in need, I'd try to come
as soon as possible. And yet by rail
it still would take a day to reach your room.

If I should suddenly hear that you were ill
your letter would have taken a day to come.
You might be dead before I had the mail
or die the day I travelled to your room.

And if I were unexpectedly taken ill,
I wouldn't write and trouble you to come
because I know you couldn't help, nor fail
to worry in your dark and curtained room.

This is our friendship. But still
you fled, maybe from this, and must have come
to fidget round some sleazy digs or jail
somewhere unknown. Or lie dead in your room.

You used to turn up suddenly with a will
in any old street. I miss the way you'd come,
that duffel winged out like a hawk, to hail
me through the traffic. Now streets are dumb.

FARE WELL

You leave no address, vanish without trace
and sometimes I think I'd like to see you back
because I can no longer picture your face
and that cravat still falling slack.

There's only absences and spaces here
to conjure you up: gaps in the bookcase,
one sweater missing, pounds pilfered for beer
that night you burgled the place.

And memory lies. Nearly all those gaps
commemorate some row and your defence
a blindly drunken evening, then collapse
and days spent hunting up pence.

The works of Synge, your austere countryman,
the plays of Shakspere. Dunbar gone, too,
I notice now as once again I scan
the shelves, thinking of you.

So unpredictable you are I cannot say,
but if it's gone your road, I think you took
The Lament of the Makaris, one day,
not the whole book.

For you had names to fill another list:
people you used to know, the towns you fled.
Once over your brew of tea you gave the gist
as it came into your head.

Discarded now, those books have fallen behind
in lodgings you left long since. And anyhow
that address upon the flyleaf will not find
the house I live in now.

THINKING OF WRITING A LETTER

Now if I had your address what could I write?
I've seen the shots a cancer patient needs
towards the end. You drift incurably ill,
and your suffering must be worse, the drugs you take.

So I could say it's raining here tonight,
confide I sometimes wake shivering in beads
of sweat to think I have no means to kill
myself, no pills—only knives, the quarry lake.

And they need courage. Some comrade I'd make
in your despair. So I suppose I'd fill
some sheets with quotes, a rhyme, retort or slight
to draw you on to cap one of my leads.

And you would quote again that Yeats you take
to justify your ways beyond your skill.
Something like: *Whatever flames upon the night*
Man's own resinous heart has fed; it reads.

I see England mapped before me, dark and still,
and for a moment point after point of light
from every room you ever left succeeds
across it. The last melts out like a flake.

For twenty miles around there is no hill.
Time past for beacons that can reach your sight.
The silence of this water; jagged reeds;
shatters of light that lazytong the lake.

Dear Murphy,

THE MONTHS

WINTER

All day I teach the children how thoughts are phrased.
I tell them there is beauty in our lives.
Across the playing fields the amber leaves
shine old-gold through the frost.

But as the bus fills with their noise
I gather my coat around me
hoping none will call me sir
and so transfer those looks to kill.
Snow and the leaves falling together.

The kids alight.
Then voices call attention
to a raincoat left behind.

I hear
but don't suggest I'll take it
to hand back to her next day at school.

I shiver to recall some trip or other
I wept for something left behind as a child.
Winter's not cold enough to make her chilled.
Snow and the leaves falling together.

Then I re-live the past week-end with her
sprawled like an old dress on the bed in tears.
And I with no tears to watch made for the stairs.

The draggled coat lies here.

HOUSE-MARTINS

Martins have built their nest
beneath the eaves of the house opposite.
Our bedroom window gives directly on the nest
delicately made of hanging, storeyed mud.

The fledglings shuffle there.
Sometimes she sees them
when she goes upstairs to exercise
and her shrilling call
scares me up to her to see.
All beaks and hair.

Dawn
and their squabbling chatter
irritates me sharply out of sleep
and the day starts
while she sleeps soundly as the child in her
and never seems to hear.

The fledglings will be flown
in a few weeks and then
the child awakes.

Some days
they interrupt so much
I feel I'd like the nest to fall.

THRUSH

All day that thrush divebombs the basking cat.
She must have nested in the nearby larches.
Soon she is bound to be caught,
head featherless already from its clutches.
Those silent claws will knock
her powerdive for six once they time it right.
That cry like the brake on a freight
jolts me. I'm sick of that bald, ridiculous neck.

Dawnlight hatches her cheeks with shadow lashes.
Thinking I'm still asleep she draws my fist
to feel how well her flesh
is hummocked with child. I let her, playing fast
asleep and don't unclench
my hand. She claws my fingers over her bared
stomach. They feel a bird
as though caught in the hand tremble and flinch. . .

Gazing out of the window above my desk
I start as something plummets from the eaves
close to the glass in the dusk.
A tile, I think, tensed for the thud as it dives.
But a thrush mounts up in flight,
beats down the garden, banks to miss the trees
and greys into night without trace.
Still tense for the thud I sit till quite late.

HAWK

Some hawk, surely, in wait
an hour now for homing martins, hunched
black on the gable. (One inched
up sideways on the gutter, then it quit.)

They squawk and gibber, hedge-
hop pavement weeds. Their sleights of wing astound.
One glides and underwings extend
wood-ember white. Another skims the ridge.

Hawk does not stir,
head dropped between its shoulders in a cringe.
Their aerobatics out of range,
distract themselves but not that brooding stare.

I ought to hurl a stone
and scare it, yet I keep on glancing up
expecting the black bolt to drop
upon its quarry with the force to stun.

A distrait martin homes.
Hawk drops . . . A toddler runs across the beds
to catch a feather from the birds
that always dodge around his wooden arms.

RIVER-GARDEN

She sits drinking tea
in the river garden,
a wing of hair
folded over her small ear.

Three packets of biscuits
she insisted on
tumbled like children's bricks
on the table here.

An eaveless tower of glass
rockets from shrubs behind her.
A pigeon comes to perch
upon her shoulder.

Across the tin table
a spring-heeled sparrow
bounces
in its search.

She breaks a biscuit
to draw them all around.
One of the bricks
already crumbles away.

She tries to aim the crumbs
at cheeky sparrows
but pigeons gather
and mill about the tray.

Another brick gone.
Now for the last.
Ornithosis. Bird-shit.
Germ-riddled claws.

Useless to speak or say
she shouldn't feed them crumbs
because of swellings
they may cause.

Matchstick city clerks
stride to their trains
important
in their hurry home.

They glare in passing
at two provincials
who feed everyday pigeons
and block the thoroughfare.

BATS

Eight months gone
                    obsessed with birds
at dusk she calls me to the window bay
to glimpse the fledglings trying out their wings
in grotesque flight
                    in our room
reflected by the lamps.

                        But they are bats.
Though since her mind is turned to omens
and the oldwives' tales she's heard
I do not speak.
The cry of bats is tuned beyond our hearing
but a child's is not so hard.

THE RITES

For nine months
I watched my speck of love
enlarge and grow enormous
in the great lens of your belly
till your sleep was broken
by the burden in your lap.

You wanted me
to watch you giving birth;
you said it was a bond between us
your body labouring.
But I knew my work would take me
two hundred miles away that week.

Unable to help
watching pain cram your loins
I'd stand by
cornered in our cramped room
taking your pulse in the doctor's way
and dear you softly as you choked
for gas, not air.

Your fingers
in their pain clutching my wrist
would gain a hold on me
I could not wrest away in dreams or rows.
The butting head that splits you
bears features I once had.

Initiate
of a secret society now
you murmur parturition rites I cannot know,
the breaking of the waters.
And tonight you rest these miles distant;
your time about my wrist.

CHARGES

LULLABY

Midges fizz in the dusk,
sky shows through a thin edge of moon,
a bit of honesty.

The night's a dark promise.
I can come no further with you now;
child, you must sleep.

STEPS

I glance in at the open door
to see if my light disturbs you,
head and shoulders out of the covers,
abandoned, comfortable.

The sleeping beauty of children—
my mother's comment
gushes over my childish head,
stalls my shadow on the floor.

On the bottom step of light
I'll try not to figure in your dream.
I inch the door to.
Sudden dark might wake you.

STARTING YOUR TRAVELS

You try to outstare the journeying dark
but lights burst in heliographs that blind
your sleep-disfocused eyes:
a row of uprights falling to a car's
raking beams—like dominoes in file
or ranks in a cross-fire.

The twin booms of light splinter like bars
of glass across your eyes. You look aside:
a horde of maneuvring lights,
some market town in cover of the scarp.
That embrous mercury haze across the night
the way our route must lie.

Yet rest now, child. I see shapes in the stars.
And when you wake from dream in a few nights
for terror of the light
closing in round you from the black-moss dark
I shall know how to comfort you in time
and it shall comfort you in time.

AUTUMN

The pale mauving flame
of the autumn crocus.

I take your hand to show you.
You pull it off by the bloom.

Its colours will last, child,
a little while.
We shall soon see how long.

DAMAGES

Red-admiral flickering by the cherry tree.
I saw those markings last when still a boy
and shout too sharply perhaps for you to see—
afraid insecticides may soon destroy
the last before you see your first one drift
among the phlox and sideslip, dither, lift.

And, dropping toys, you hurry to my room
fearfully fast and stand almost in tears.
(It's darning up the garden, bloom to bloom.)
I point and out you dart. It nears then veers,
now poises like a gnomon. Caught in the end.
You bring it me dead; its wings I cannot mend.

Thwarted, I try to explain calmly, brush
the vivid dust from your hands. Still you insist
it fly again, persist and will not hush
until my angry tone conveys the gist
of death. Silenced, you give me the crumpled wings.
I shelve them with your heap of broken things.

But not till bedtime dare you bring a car,
Buick *Riviera* with plastic conduction lights,
dropped when I called you on its towing bar.
You have the pieces. I say I'll put it right.
The tears delayed this morning drop as I take
the glowing plastic glue will turn opaque.

Sleep well . . .
    Your toys, my books cobble the floors.
There's that Lagonda I bought myself as a boy.
Toys to repair clutter my desk and drawers.
Irreparably damaged some you most enjoy.
Here since you insist on repairs. Instead
my words and promises litter your head.

Your strength beyond your skills, so fast you grow;
I cannot clear the backlog of things you break.
More complex now your gifts; already though,
technology in your toys outstrips me. I make
this pile, your broken marvels, forgotten, outgrown.
My words and ways you may not so simply disown.

THE GOING

WAIT AND SEE

This is the bar you said where we could meet.
I take the corner opposite the door,
prepared to wait
and half-resigned to sit
with one glass for an hour.

Each time a figure darkens the window
I watch the door. And for a moment
a head takes on that bob of yours,
a leg your casual lope,
and I am drawn by you
to several other women.

TANGIBLES

It was one of those crisp autumn days,
you said,
as if they were consecutive,
distinct yet somehow comparable
as the misty shimmer in each pearl
around your throat.
And so I remember it was—
the crack of apple,
the tang of juice in the teeth
and your hands
always cold at first touch.

COUNTRY WALK

I've wound it many times
around my fingers,
that scroll of your hair
fumbled over by the breeze.
It will carry these buttercups
and more.

Masses of buttercups
blacken the grass
until we walk unsteadily
a sky of shaking stars.

Down to earth
in our old spinney,
the sun a hole charred in the boughs,
you reach across me
seeking a leaf of every green
till I catch
in the tips of your hair
a spectrum of stars.

THE SWIFTS

The swifts are back,
their flight on a knife-edge.
In the dusk we watch them
and feel at peace.
Their grace we take
as confirmation.

Our swifts are back,
we say, and touch now.
But their grace survives them,
whichever were ours.
And it hurts to touch you,
that wing of hair.

Whose love, my love,
in my hands tonight?
Whose spring again
in the bounce of your hair?
Our love is ghosted;
our swifts return.

SILVER BIRCH

A delicacy of white feathers
that can cut the hand
rising out of the mist.
One bough the leading edge
of a swan's wing raised for flight.

My hands could span the trunk
arched into darkness
like your throat
thrown back in love.

One dusk when mist returns
walk along this way, love,
gather an inkling,
my angle of you,
your head thrown back.

PRESENCE

Shadow of a bird in flight
across my window
jogs my room like a blink.

A whole train of thought gone
as though you with your quiet
had come in and sat down.

RETURNS

A few silver birches among dark pines
like frozen lightnings. They take us back.

You tried to match your steps to my prints
in the soft earth here, such strides.
You pranced in those days. But look,
I cannot tread again in my last print.
A minute edge crumbles like those cliffs
at Cromer where we walked ten years ago.

The going loosens. I take your wrist once more.
White pressure of my grip expands
more or less the same as when you first
stumbled on these tracks
although I cannot touch you quite again
where once I held you fast.

We cover the same gound.
Your life fits into mine.

DUSK

Moon a sliver of apple
blue on a knife-blade.

Light enough for a known face.
I touch shadow round your eyes.

GIFT OF WORDS

That patience of yours,
standing half the morning
to watch a rose you planted bloom.

So long like that, years,
you've waited for me.
I have to watch you always.

Crescent of melon, your bare back
where blouse and jeans have come apart.
The windows between us.

Too impatient to watch your roses,
I want my hands to feel
the equipoise of your hips.

You turn with a spray of roses,
a focus for my room,
fragrant cloud, I think you call them.

The petals will drop silently for days
scented on these files and folders.
Sometimes I've heard them land.

CROCUS

Our old gnarled path.
We're late again this year,
the still flame in our clump
of crocus past its best,
but one, sculptured, fragile,
half an eggshell.

Your head to one side,
your hair heavy and slow,
my plumb-line,
sways to the vertical
as you kneel and try
to purse it up to flame again.

SLEEP

As soon as your sleep is sound
I slip my arm from around you.
You can't tell
though you'll dream something up
to explain your loss of warmth.

In the still hours
your cold hands reach for me.
Their gentle pressure
hardly disturbs my sleep.
Unstirring, they become my warmth.

LULLABY

Sleep, love, go to sleep
and I'll watch over you
as I have done these years,
these shadows of curtain haze,
and breathe into your hair
the things we do not say.

You murmur as if you hear
some saying of the day,
and nuzzle the pillow down
but tracing an edge of light
along your shoulder line
my hands touch on your dream.

HOLD

That perfect apse
your fingers with their curvature.
They hold a stillness
I can’t touch.

Tentative,
your hands sense out
for things as if air
lay denser round them.

Mine
that undo things for you
would leave their mark.

Love,
it’s not much
but it’s something
we hold together.

LOST AND FOUND

The warmth of her, unbreathable
as she presses over me
hopelessly scanning the shelves
the only way she knows.

(She asked the time on Westminster Bridge.)
She turns the plants to the sun
and she is looking for a map of the district.
I round on her—like a moth.

OLD HAUNT

Scotch fir, the trunk
staked in the still pools of its boughs
on the old hill.

The needles kill the grass
where we left our shapes
so long ago.

Its criss-crossings
crazed your bare legs.
You tried for a fern pattern.

This stillness was there then;
boughs like green snow overhanging;
and the peace was no trouble to us.

DIRECTIONS

No way between us
but the worm's, these casts,
a few cropped stalks
that tick as we shift
our rigid positions.

I've green fingers at last:
can raise a few
hollow stalks
in the sun-crazed earth.
A word could reach you.

Hard to say,
and you attuned
to the grey gulls
silver to seaward.
Hard to tell which.

If I raised my hand
towards them
its shadow would touch you
more lightly than my love.
You'd notice that.

There, it blocks your sun.

GULL

Gull, is it?
skims across the glare.
"Me, I can follow it,"
you cry: "Another language
over there; another life."

I shield your eyesight from the sun.
"Your hand's on fire, the blood's alight.
Clench it, clench your fist—
this one is flying high."

Sun penetrates your lids.
Both fists clenched to your eyes,
your head swings back to me,
elbows and wrists your skeletal wings

TWO SPARROWS

They take off squabbling
and loop each other
like a flying bolas—
and their brief shadows.

Time to see it happen:
our hands likc that now
when they skirmish to maneuvre
in open tenderness.

GIFTS

More books,
that dress I thought was you,
worn once,
another pen to try my hand.

We're down to gifts now,
mine against yours,
and each more costly than the last.

They hang fire about us everywhere.

MEANDER

Dark meander of hair
a river between banks of snow
and my touch lasting
like a snowflake in its course.

KEEPER

Something about you that might break,
a hand's turn
delicate as a figurine,
caught and held me.

Something small and terrified
sheltered in the verve of your eyes
like a silver fox,
nocturnal, svelte.

A lull in the talk,
the dark suddenly noticeable
and the odd glance
of something too timid to tame.

The sight grows rarer, love.
It keeps more and more from me.
My old nightfarer,
let it still live.

RETROSPECT

Wanting some yourself
you offer me cherries.
Girlish again
you hang a pair over your ear
pale where they touched
as your breasts were.

Wanting memories
you hold out a wishbone stalk
to split between us.

But I want my time back.
Give me back
the pressure of my hands.

TIE

A marbling of fine veins
across your right temple,
the skin opalescent.
Blood too near the surface.

TRUCE

In your play which was no play
the knife glanced my arm,
a red mouth opened mute.

A fortnight's casual conversation
out of that
now healed to a scar.

TWILIGHT

Dusk
lit by a bowl of roses
and your hand white, so white
against the oak table,
poses a peace I know only by sight.

Dark to you always
my hands seemed closer once
than nocturnes in black and white
those nights your shoulders gleamed,
that mane of shadow down your back.

DEADLOCK

Nothing more irritating
when the hands are engaged
than a trickle of liquid
like an insect running down the face,
rain or sweat or even blood.

You want me to take your hand in mine
and will not want to dry your eyes
until I do,
though I will wait
until you fall asleep.

IMPASSE

Your eyes closed on me.
Your drift always against my drive.
I draw your scalp back by the hair
to lift the lids.

And by the time they do
I shall have gritted my teeth
into a smile for you.

RETRACTION

Your overnight bag gone;
so much left behind:
you tried to keep everything.

I go over again in black
the words I wrote you
or underscored in red.

The flourishes defeat me,
the dab hand
has lost its cunning.

The red shows through.
I'll send them on.
Retraction enough.

INSIGHT

For sight like an ophthalmoscope,
once it was a wish
now what a hope
to penetrate the leaf-light
of your green iris
to the shadowplay beyond.

The dark can take you now
for all a shaft could show:
a room of gipsy flowers
and potted plants,
the ten-mirror echo
of your defensive laugh.

KEEPSAKE

You call me to you
kneeling over a single crocus
under the oak.

Your scroll of hair
now screening the steady flame,
some secret you'd have unique:

These three impressures
inset within the petal,
fluted, concave, minute.

How long we'd keep this insight in season,
you said,
as ours, strong as a vow.

But I have held that moment:
you leaning,
your hair scrolled around your shoulders . . .

And now this clump of crocus
hidden a moment in time,
its saffron blinding.

THE MIND'S EYE

Curls that should jingle with your slightest move—
I might have known you'd soon be back,
your next shift
to trouble the mind's eye.

Naked, or dressed to kill.
But clothed—that's new.
I watch the passes that you make,
your hands slow-motioning to save a glass.

Your skirt deflating like a parachute,
you kneel and tilt your head
to catch the glint of fragments littering the floor.

That skirt's a laugh,
and just to pique you more
I'm going to make you last like that
and unaware before me on your knees.

Those curls will jingle at your slightest move—
After-image, my after-love, look up.
You're still my only source of feeling.

EIDETIC IMAGE

Memory of a girl laughing,
your hair a fall of flame,
gold burning down
and shadow flickering up,
head to one side
like a bird listening.

Pose of an advert now—
mirror enough for you at last—
you get at me from all angles.

I don't know how widespread you are
but I expect you everywhere.
And at this distance alone reflect—
nostalgia if you like—
that maybe you've never posed this one before,
a girl laughing in her glass
without your famous poise,
the shadow flickering up,
the gold burning down.

OBSESSION

I bear you in mind always—white
as balsa wood your body was.
You were all women once to me.

That blade of shadow down your thigh,
it's pretty common; some of your ways
I love in every woman I meet.

I've assembled all of them tonight,
all dressed to kill and all to watch
your private strip; it's your big scene.

I bare you in the mind's eye
so make it hot and strong for once;
they'll take your fine points off, my sweet.

VIGIL

Now you are gone
your small perfections inveigle me:
curve of your eyelid closed in sleep
widens to my horizon.

Sleepless
I used to watch those pupils move,
shifting deltas of blue veins,
blindly scanning my face.

Some nights I came near
my lips in touch
with your pulsing lids
to catch the drift of your dream.

WILDFLOWER

Crushed fragrance
and a few flowerheads
bend to the light
out of my footprints—
purple florets,
established, wild,
encroaching underfoot.

How long ago it must have been
you told me the local name
for something much like this,
if I remember it,
in those days
when what your hands touched
was my life.

THE YEARS

EVANESCENCE

Dark blocks
of houses that loom up
out of the fog and powder off.

For one bird
that stays on the bare shrub,
grateful as I pass its perch.

FULL CIRCLE

Same book. Last year the reader's throat grew dry,
the meaning garbled till the mood was lost
on all the rest in boredom. This time I'll read
the ending out: the prison-ship is tossed
against the rocks of home; one friend must die
saving the younger just as both are freed
from chains by storm to grasp the chain of hands
that friends reach out across the years and sands.

"Greater love . . ." Yes. Even that quote.
The faithful girl has kept a flame lit there
for seamen in such straits. Now home, the dead
hero is laid out on the table where
he once had laid his son in death. And note:
the son adopted mourns the father dead—
a careful symmetry. And one attends
them, greyhaired now, not knowing his old friends.

I ham it up. The seniors I overlook
glance up from private study, grin: the course
they did two years ago. They catch my eye
but other eyes are reddened by the force
of words and blinkered by tears to the book
for hero's death when nearly home and dry,
for one after long exile returned. Neat,
unlikely, a vicious circle so complete.

Lump in the throat. Yet not for hero friends,
still less for home that circles round once more,
nor for the woman who could wait so long
for love; but for impossibilities of this order,
coincidences necessary to shape these ends
—seniors listening now—for kids so strongly
moved by some shape of life prefigured there.
The seniors know already it will not wear.

Finis. And silence. I must break this spell.
Seniors laugh off the mood remembered, lame
laughter the kids can hardly understand.
Try questions. No one speaks. Pick on a name.
A laugher or a quiet one? The bell.
And out they file too quietly. A handful
of seniors asks how many times the book
comes round. Half-smiling, I answer with a look.

TERRACE

A terrace of tulips
colourful as a crowd.
What they need
is a match to watch.

Will this old tabby do
sleeping in the sun?

EIGHTH PERIOD

Last year's sexkitten, out of work again,
(mean effrontress, chased and bare)
saunters about the grounds with her Great Dane
as sandy blonde as that lassitude of hair—
boy-hunting, leash seductively in hand.
Four o'clock and time to make a stand.

I plot my progress through the room to reach
the window for a glimpse of her, compare
her insinuity with these hulks I teach,
mobile jumble-sales with sweep's brush hair.
One week to go. Difficult to think
by then they'll learn to dress like her and slink.

Drama for Today. She reads a speech,
a mother deprived of husband and only son
in the World War. (Once more undo her breach,
dear friends.) The long day's task is done.
The slumping class as usual does not hear,
luckily. She speaks with passion. And they'd jeer.

Only I hear and follow closely now,
head in the book to hide my smarting eyes,
tensing for fear I have to pick a row
with some lout there before that passion dies.
This part of her may last until the bell,
perhaps a year. A glance outside may tell.

Unhindered sunset across the silt plain
leans in the window deriding all shapes,
knocking the shadows sideways once again.
Chalk dust solidifies two broken scapes
of light propped on the sill. Some day soon
that girl will find her shadow squat at noon.

And this one? She'll leave now that she can
to work for drinks, good lays and a night's rest.
And then she'll feel it in her bones how man
is easy straight up or flat out at best;
till at her gate one evening she will stand
watching his shadow deformed by ploughed land.

SUMMER

Clouds shift; the shadows fall.
Stallion-gloss of sunlight
on a bough-back.

Clouds shift; the leaves rustle.
I wait for that sunshaft
to light there again.

SINGLE TICKET

The train rattles through the night.
That face opposite. More sallow now
yet still that hair mists into light,
the skin more mobile on the brow,
a lapse of memory. Or time.
Gone that sidelong
glance her eyes had, green as lime.
Caught in scrutiny of a face
they lowered like a dog's in disgrace.
Now tears rim those eyes once strong.

Time and again she glances my way.
Unsure, I wonder whether she tries
to place me or returns the stray
stares I prolong to recognize
her features. I turn to the dusty pane
and there's her face
wrinkled and weeping in the driving rain.
Illness or years might make her look
like this. I nod back to my book
returning through years to the old place.

A trick of memory, commonsense
insists. There's a ring on her hand.
Too much depends on coincidence
for one homecoming in years to land
me on this branch of the local line
in the same train
with her, however changed those fine
features, the laughter corded round
the lips. I stare again as if bound
to catch some trait clinchingly plain.

That battered case offers no clue,
no name, no label. Travelling alone
she troubles me like one I knew
by sight those years ago, the tone
of her voice unheard. I do not speak
and nor does she.
If we'd once broken week after week
of this we might have joined this train
together, and her eyes not show such pain.
I doubt it, though. She stares at me.

My stop. She gets out further down
the corridor and runs as once she ran
when late to catch her train to town—
or any woman runs to dodge a man
who eyes her too intently. I walk
the other way
and two miles home rehearsing talk
to come. Her heels tick into night.
More faces to re-shape at sight,
their recognitions to outstare next day.

NOT DRINKING WATER

Home after years, tonight,
cleaning my teeth,
I taste the waters of childhood,
still unfluorided,
tangless, not tepid, quite—
once an apple-slicing chill
by which all quenchings could be placed.

Suddenly minute fear, not noticing
the granary tower by the old mill pond
that used to dominate the sky round here—
dwarfed
a little beyond
some concrete block for storing flour.

I've tasted many waters,
mineralled, full of lime,
brine of the eyes,
the sweat of her brow,
hard and soft and somewhere bitter.
This taste I seem to forget.
I have been thirsty all my life.

OVER-NIGHT COACH

Shot with sleep the head slumps on the chest.
Ribs jolt against me every corner swing.

But I don't know your name or anything
thought my shoulder would afford some kind of rest.

I sit in arm's reach to cushion your back
but you have to lean against a travel bag.

And yet I stay awake in case you sag
for then my hand could save your head a crack.

I watch the branches tearing great rents
across your face projected as if dead.

And if I cannot shoulder your sleeping head
it is because time comes I may not raise

your bowed head from its tears. The road strays
briefly through England. And there are continents.

PRE-OCCUPATIONS

Saboteurs, three women, who have killed
men of the occupation, they rifle down
at point blank range, ordered in cold
blood in the dawn.

Straight in our living room the rifles aim
and you lounged there on your calves, thighs taut,
but I could never reach the switch in time,
let alone fight it out.

Longer on film, though, unnerving to sit and watch.
A frame of levelled barrels; defiant rod
of muscle down the throat. Could reach and switch
it off. But the guns roared.

Time for heroics. Last frame the flash
and crack of guns. Several shots I heard.
The women? No sign of violated flesh.
You turn away your head.

Dead now, and tidier, slightly, than the troops
their bombs quartered. Nothing could be done.
And I could never gun them down nor traipse
to death with them at dawn.

But squad marches to breakfast in a burst of sun,
a routine duty done without thought or anger.
And that rod of muscle down her throat, a sign
not of defiance but hunger.

Time for commercials now and things are safer.
Sunshine breakfast food for growing boys.
Beer for men. These messages need no cipher
and the public obeys.

I can't defend you, islands of my flesh,
from subversion on the streets and on the beaches
with any Churchillian rhetoric. Sunburst flash:
The News: Vietnam.

LEAF

Chestnut leaf
trodden like a transfer
into the pavement.

All night it rains
and in the morning nothing's left
but an ochre stain.

I count on that tinge a week
before I lose the place
on the grey stones.

THE SIGNATURE

I stare beyond the walls of glass.
No sound but pens in the busy class.

Restless, I walk along the aisle
to watch them trying letter-style.

And then one asks me
how to sign a letter to his father.

Mine has been dead years
yet I cannot bring myself to speak the words.

I ring 'Yours faithfully,'
and yet above I cannot write:

'Love . . .'

IT IS FINISHED

IT IS FINISHED

Not cramp that makes you laugh and cry at once.
Something quite different. Then one day it hurt.
It hurt all day, that night, a week and now.
That took some getting used to but after a while
it was just there hovering in the back of the mind,
recalled by sudden movement once in a way.

Soon I could hear people talking again,
their careless use of the third person, watch
the social smiles poising, delicate
as balances swayed in the least wind of talk.
Then it hurt more and I couldn't stand them there.
They had to come. I wanted them to go,
zip up their chinking teeth and let me be.
I felt so small. The room loomed huge
and pain held most of me except the bare
bulb in the mind round which I flickered like
a moth gyrating round and round its death.

Hospital. They gave me something drugged
so I would feel all right and then that night
I had a good sleep, the best for months,
only I dreamt of a wound slashed apart
like a pomegranate. Not too pleasant, that.
Well, if I groan too loud that probationer
runs from her doze to tend my sleeplessness.
Not that she can do much. And so I try
not to disturb her. One day I will be
her first death. After the first death
there is no other. It should be a loved one.
Seldom these days. She won't forget my face.
She's got a sense of humour, used to come
and zing the blinds up just to waken you.
She was too nice to shout you out of sleep.
I used to make out I was like a log.
She'd come across and with her icy hands
and rasp-like finger-tips she'd chill my face.
I used to like that, her hair swaying down.

She knows I'm dying, hasn't learnt the way
to hide such things. Too young. She rarely comes
at odd moments now. Embarrassed I suppose
to make small talk with death upon the mind,
afraid I'll writhe in mid-remark to her.
That scares me too, though not so she would know.
I seldom call her but she waits on me,
and me, I wait on death. I have to wait.
I think about it sometimes, passes an hour.
Just what you need lying here, a big thought.
Some visitors come and ask you how you are.
You lie to them, they smile and lie to you,
embarrassed also like my little nurse.
My son, my son, why should you visit me?
The trains take hours, the buses days to come.
Your time's your own; why give it me to waste.
My life was before you and yours after mine.
I've given you your independence, this
will seal the deed and I will leave you free.
We have no words to bridge such times with minds.
Here are *The Sonnets*. The parts I've underlined
I leave with you. Richard's my man now.
He had the better way to make an end;
he died a king. But I am not the first
of fortune's slaves and shall not be the last
for many have and others must lie here
and in this thought I find a sort of ease.
That's the real worry: how to die a man
with, say, a little dignity to go on.
It must be terrible to watch a coward die.
I must die quiet. Why should my little nurse
remember this old face in death for life?
Too mild in life to speak your mind at all,
you'll be too shy to shriek with pain at last.
If the mind holds but they've got drugs now.
You thought my silence strength of mind outside.
It's too late now to speak. Uncomfortable,
being afraid. But what of heroes then?

Most of them bloody fools, a waste of breath.
Try Nurse Cavell. Better than Nightingale.
(I have been half in love with easeful death.)
My little nurse is neither. Cavell then.
You never hear the shot that does you in.
So rapid there's no time to hate or shriek.
This is better although her thoughts are mine.
So this is it. I wonder what it's like.
It's what we all are aiming for in time.
Grow old along with me. The best is yet
to be. Or not . . .

The best has been and not
enough repeated: the soft innermost thrust
through layered undermushroom textures home.
Ah, that's the bell to clear the visitors.
I've lived my life to bells like a bus-driver.
These flowers still smell good. Prefer them wild.
The fluted thigh, tongue-to-palate touch
of rose-petals, and her mouth like that once.
At least this pain is something to fight against.
No one can fight a firing squad, you know.
There's no rush to think of something to bite on.
I am powerless against no one I hate;
I'm not helpless quite, so it's not too bad.
Good night my son, sleep tight. I'll be all right.
See, I can reach the water by myself.
Paradise would be a drink that satisfied
the thirst and yet was interesting to taste.
Water does one but bores, and all my life
I tried to find a drink that would do both.
Now I am going a long journey
and would like something to drink,
not that I thirst . . .

LAST RESPECTS

I know these hands, their feel,
knew of the cuts beneath the scars
and wondered when the split nail would heal.

They used to lark
with birds of shadow on the wall
for children scared of the dark.

Fall now—
and all the birds are flown.

Hunched shadows black the wall.

FRAGMENTS

Alas 't is true, I have gone here and there
And made myself a motley to the view,
Gored mine own thoughts, sold cheap what is most dear,
Made old offences of affections new.
Most true it is, that I have looked on truth
Askance and strangely . . .

So they've returned the book of verse
I gave you. It stands narrow among mine,
gold-lettered in the paperbacks and plain
covers. Thin. But you were always terse.
I seldom read a line
but verses now and again
come by me. Sometimes your words fill my head;
they speak of my desires but yours the voice.
I try to fade them out now you are dead.
Your library not my choice.

6,000,000 Guinness drunk every day. . .

SELECTED POEMS

THE STORMS

Losing my patience setting type in the press
you gave me I can hear your voice insist
Paul was no artist since he would untwist
knots you'd snip and slash. Such pithiness
from you, thought worthy once to break a spell
of silence, startles me and I recall
how far away you are, crowding with all
your work into a room in Camberwell.

Once as I walked with your usual silent self
you spoke out: A bag of peanuts equals the weight
of Boehme's works; your pockets bulged with great
wisdom but meagre food . . .
                                        Here on the shelf
your Boehme lies. Thumbprints of paint edge
your favourite lines. They mark my books you read,
snatched in frenzy to back something you said,
or rammed beneath your easel as a wedge.

Outside the study window now the tree
I tried describing, you to draw, is a flare
of shuffling leaves. All that's left of the bare
boughs are my words and these two or three
sketches recalling how your hands would form
a winterstruck tree whenever you discussed
the way you start a carving. A slight gust
rustles the leaves but ushers in no storm.

Rainbow's trajectory zooms over the scarp
shoulder plunging straight upon the town
huddled beneath the shelter of the down.
And I think of other trajectories, your sharp
erratic course through towns; sketches that lie
discarded in lodgings like a paper trail
no one can track; this tree you traced as a frail
skeletal hand to close against the sky.

The leaves will motley soon ready to drop.
The first winds will flail the branches bare.
I set alight the sketches I kept, they flare,
darken and gnarl. You could come and stop
the winter. Then perhaps your hands would rouse
to shape this tree again. The slate light
wouldn't disturb your photophobic sight.
Come and bring your storm into my house.

The window casts a broken shaft of light
towards the darkness. The valley lights wink out
one at a time. Your tree rustles about
my shadowed head. This lamp is seen for quite
a distance. But not by you. Nothing can find
you in that darkness where your sketches sail
like papers from a house ransacked by gale.
Come back for the storm beats into my mind.

I stare my face out, glad that some have sworn
us relatives. Your nose is longer, your lips
curve with the sensuous line of women's hips,
mine are a scar. And brothers, I know, are born
of one woman's suffering. Yet I have led
your wandering life with you and I have known
your hands gnarl into a tree of bone.
And tonight your storm beats into my head.

Last light vanishes. Cold night air creeps
under the doors and windows, up my back.
Wind begins to rush and with a crack
the branches sway. A single leaf sweeps
against the pane, a moth the glass deceives.
Rain beats like canvas tearing. I draw
the blinds across the distorted face I saw.
Take shelter. Late birds bicker in the eaves.

TRANSATLANTIC
(for Wallace Kaufman)

Glimpse of a street urchin with that same
brush-cut hair leaning stiff off his brow
like grass that overhangs a cliff. And now
I almost call your name.

The things that remind of you. The model guy
in ads for Hepworth suits can jerk his chin
out, tilt his head with just your perky grin
and your alert bird-eye.

And every now and then these distant miles
from where we once had rooms, I find your scrawl
turning up still on notes to remind me you'd call—
folded in books or files.

But you? I know you. You used to walk
off to strange pubs to chat and joke with new
faces, the broads, bums, drunks, your local view,
as we drank missing your talk.

I know you. You're in some joint no one knows.
Three thousand miles or so of sea won't make
much difference to you. And three streets take
you several miles I suppose.

I hear the infinity of waters boom
on Roman-numeral struts of the landing stage.
Trees awash with wind, this hand on the page
and your seas flood my room.

OBTAINABLE AT ALL GOOD HERBALISTS

The eyes of your trinket laughter
are with me, they dance in the street,
like moon-skittering water,
I can hardly walk straight.

Oh what shall I do
with all these lights on route?
They will not distil a dew
to necklace your bright throat.

Hesitant, I halt
outside the herbalist's
for purslane and burdock held
to lengthen our lives and lusts.

Half-humorously I scan
the galleonate window bay:
julep, moly to gloss the skin.
Almost I enter and buy.

Yet, if I bought a phial,
some glass-blower's masterpiece,
your health and joy to taste and feel,
that after as a vase would pass—

A careless wave of ease,
twin crescents of your laughter
would flaunt me out of face
and you would drink plain water.

Sleek one, cultivate cats
with latex tongue and suede nose
for their flattering slinky coats.
Witch, you've taken my wits with your knees.

CROWD

Come away from crowds,
you fool,
why do you hang about?
If she should turn up now
she would be old.

That one is like her, dark,
long hair,
strong stride, unshaken calf . . .
Unfaithful eye,
recharge the mind.

RECOGNITION

Face once loved
so constant in the mind
I could have passed you anywhere
not knowing who you were.

OLD POET ON A RAINY DAY

for David Jones

My old acquaintances and peers
once allied in the lonely art
and rivals in our riper years
gather together now on shelves
after so sure a life apart
and peace becomes their books, themselves.

TRANSLATIONS

VILLON'S EPITAPH

Brothers that live when we are dead,
don't set yourselves against us too.
If you could pity us instead
then God will sooner pity you.
We five or six strung up to view,
dangling the flesh we fed so well,
are eaten piecemeal, rot and smell.
We bones in a fine dust shall fall.
No one make that a laugh to tell:
pray God may save us one and all.

Brothers, if that's the word we said,
it's no disparagement to you
although in justice we hang dead.
Yet all the same you know how few
are men of sense in all they do.
Pray now we're dead that Jesu's well
of grace shall not run dry—nor Hell
open in thunder as we fall.
We're dead; don't harry us as well:
pray God may save us one and all.

Showered and rinsed with rain, we dead
the sun has dried out black and blue.
Magpie and crow gouge out each head
for eyes and pluck the hairs. On view,
never at rest a moment or two,
winds blow us here or there a spell;
more pricked than a tailor's thumb could tell
we're needled by the birds. Don't fall
then for our brotherhood and cell:
pray God may save us one and all.

Prince, Lord of Men, oh keep us well
beyond the sovereignty of Hell.
On him we've no business to call.
And, men, it's no joke now I tell:
pray God may save us one and all.

HOMAGE TO THE COURT

(Written after Parliament had commuted his death-sentence to banishment from Paris.)

All of my five senses, eyes, mouth, ears, nose
and you, old sensitive, lend your support.
All of my parts now in reproach propose,
each in its proper place, these words: ''O Court,
by whose good offices we weren't cut short,
you've saved us all from death. With one accord—
since tongue alone can't of itself afford
sufficient praise—we'll speak up as we should
together, daughter of our Sovereign Lord,
sister of angels, mother of those who're good.

Break, heart, or be run through, but don't suppose
at least you're any harder than the sort
of hard grey rock that struck by Moses flows
with water for the Jews. Weep tears, in short,
tenderly sighing, humble in heart and thought.
Extol the Court, defence of all abroad,
the joy of France, created by the Lord
in the kingdom of heaven, and by neighbourhood
joined with the Holy Empire in accord,
sister of angels, mother of those who're good.

And you, my teeth, all loose enough, God knows,
leap out and give the Court a good report,
louder than trumpet, bell or organ goes.
And as for chewing, never give it a thought.
Lights, lungs, and guts that still with me consort,
just think: we might be dead. You're not ignored,
body—more foul than swine whose bed and board
is shit—before you mess up more you should
allow the Court all praise you can afford,
sister of angels, mother of those who're good.

Prince, would you spare me three more days to sort
my things out and to say goodbye? I'm short
of cash unless I see my folks. (I'm stood
off by the changers.) *Fiat,* triumphant Court,
sister of angels, mother of those who're good.

VILLON

EVENING HARMONY

Now comes the hour when stirring on its tendril sways
each flower exhaling fragrance like a censer's swing;
perfume and sounds are drifting airs of evening;
a melancholy waltz, vertiginous, languid daze.

Each flower exhaling fragrance like a censer's swing,
a troubled heart, the trembling violin now plays
a melancholy waltz, vertiginous, languid daze.
Sky, like a greater altar, a sad and splendid thing.

A troubled heart, the trembling violin now plays,
a tender heart that hates the vast void darkening.
Sky, like a great altar, a sad and splendid thing;
the sun drowns in its own blood's congealing blaze.

A tender heart that hates the vast void darkening
culls from the past each trace of earlier, luminous days.
The sun drowns in its own blood's congealing blaze . . .
Your memory like a monstrance in me glimmering.

BAUDELAIRE

AT THE GREEN INN

A week I'd dragged the bootsoles off my feet
then came to Charleroi, the Green Inn there.
Bread, butter, and ham just cool enough to eat
I ordered, sprawled my legs without a care
at the green table and traced the artless bits
of pattern round the walls. And it was great
when this girl with lively eyes and big tits—
no kiss would scare her off, at any rate—
brought what I ordered on a coloured plate:
bread, butter, and ham not yet too cold,
ham pink and white, a touch of garlic, too;
and filled my hefty tankard with a brew
whose head rose up and caught a ray of late
sunlight that turned it instantly to gold.

RIMBAUD

ON THE ROAD

I went off, hands in pockets full of holes,
my coat grown more imaginative than made.
Under the open sky, you had my soul,
Muse, but tut, tut, the dreamgirls that I laid.

My only pair of trousers gaped with a tear.
Tom Thumb, the daydream, all along the way
I rhymed aloud. My inn was the Great Bear,
my stars would sidle with a silken sway.

I listened to them, pausing on my route
those fine September evenings when the dew
touched my forehead like reviving wine.
I rhymed away where fantastic shadows grew,
and plucked the only lyre that was mine
(one foot to my heart): elastic of my boot!

RIMBAUD

EVENING PRAYERS

I take things sitting down—angelic type
at the barber's—fluted tankard in my fist,
belly and neck curved, my Gambier pipe
filling the air with veils that lift and twist.

I'm burnt by the mild heat of a thousand dreams
like the warm droppings left within an old
dovecote. From time to time my sad heart seems
sapwood where pollen bleeds its fresh dark gold.

Now when I've bolted down my dreams, I turn
and pull myself together just to cope
with ten to fifteen jars—a need that burns.

High and far out on dark skies I piss,
sweetly as our Saviour of Cedar and Hyssop,
winning approval of great heliotropes.

RIMBAUD

from THE SEASONS OF CANKAM

poems made from classical Tamil from transcripts and notes of Kokilam Subbiah

NOTE

The poems translated here date from around 200 A.D. The tradition of Tamil poetry seems to have been very formal and conventional—too complex to explain here, even if I felt sure I had mastered it. Basically, it is something like this. The poems, after a long oral tradition, were eventually collected into eight anthologies, arranged according to length, like haikus or sonnets. Kuṟuntokai was the anthology of poems from 5-9 lines; Naṟṟinai of 9-12. The Puṟam poem comes from a different, heroic anthology, as opposed to these of subjective love lyrics. The heroic poetry provides most of the evidence of dating. All the poems share a complex form of seasonal symbolism which is known as *The Five Landscapes*, though they mostly suggest mood. These five seasons establish the stages of the man-woman relationship. The two demonstrated here are Kuṟiñci, named after a flower, the cone-head or strobilanthes; it is the season and place of lovers' meetings, for sexual union and its joys. Pālai, named after the desert wastes, implied the time and place of lovers' parting or the ordeals undergone as tests of love. These landscapes also could indicate the types of man in question since the landscape words symbolize the type of culture supported there. For example, the desert wastes supported chiefly robbers of food trains; the lakes supported a gentler fishing culture. The symbolism is widespread, obligatory and elusive. Complex, full of overtones, multivalent, it is difficult to render even when it can be detected. I have been obliged to concentrate more on the mood of the season than its externals. I believe these poems, however diminished in translation, are still able to speak for themselves.

P.D.

KUṞUNTOKAI 44

Season: Pālai

WHAT HER MOTHER SAID WHEN SHE ELOPED

I have walked and trudged
till my feet ache;
I have searched and searched
till my eyes are dim.

Surely in this wide world
it is the other couples,
not my daughter and her man,
who are indistinguishable
as the stars in the vast sky.

Veḷḷivītiyār

KUṞUNTOKAI 161

Season: Kuṟiñci

SHE SPEAKS TO HER FRIEND

There was no sun there, my friend,
I'm telling you.
Even the demons shivered in the ceaseless rains.
My mother, her son tight in her arms,
cried out more than once
despite the charm of tiger teeth
around his neck.

It was my man from the mountains,
fragrant as his local sandalwood,
standing behind our house
like a wet elephant.
What do you think he was after?

Nakkīrar

KUR̲UNTOKAI 310

Season: Kur̲iñci

WHAT SHE SAID WHEN HE DID NOT COME

The bird's last call has echoed home,
the water-lilies close,
deserted the shore.
Darkness mantles the sky.

Light and the last of my beauty
gone from the lake.

Someone go and tell my love
along the shore somewhere
how long I wait.

By the shore of this lake he lives
in the fragrance of these water-lilies.

Someone go and tell him
I am still alive.

Perunkaṇṇan̲

NAṞṞINAI: 160

Season: Kuṟiñci

HE TOLD HIS FRIEND

Noble thoughts I had,
high ideals,
considerate I was
and brave,
a man of charity like my forebears.
More so than was good for me.

That was before I caught
the proud glance of this girl
and her soft freckled breasts
with the uppish nipples.
The bounce of her coiled hair
spiralled round her golden brow!

Two liquid eyes
like new-blown water-lilies.
I'm sunk.

Anon.

PUṞAM 255

THE WIFE CRIES ON THE BATTLEFIELD

If I could only utter my tears
their echoes would wake the tiger.
Alas, it would drag you away.

If I could only raise
your broad shoulders in my arms—
too weak, too weak.

May the cursed god who let you die
suffer as much as I.

Cool shade under those hills.
Love, rise and walk with me,
hold my many-bangled hands.

Ālattūrkiḻār

VERSE PLAY

CELL

CHARACTERS

A. B.: a political prisoner in an indeterminate totalitarian modern state.

Medical Attendant: employed in the prison service.

A Priest: in attendance at the prison.

First Guard

Second Guard: both of whom are from a military detachment to the prison.

CELL: A PLAY

TIME: Indeterminate, twentieth century onward.

SCENE: A whitewashed cell that may either be medical or appear penitentiary in its sparseness and clinical cleanliness as the lights come up. Centre stage, rear, a double door into the cell made of iron and heavy. A grill and spyhole in each leaf. The shadow of the bars in the window-hole is thrown periodically throughout the play to the right of this door and sometimes partly on to the floor. Left rear stage a primitive bed and palliasse, a cupboard at the head. The scene opens in darkness with screams of human agony off-stage. The sound of a blow just as the screams appear to approach the doors. They are flung open revealing a harsh red light momentarily before very bright, clinical stage lighting takes over. Two attendants dressed in white medical gear throw a patient/prisoner into the cell and swiftly clang the doors shut. Silence. Prolonged. Fade in low sound of irregular heartbeats slowly becoming regular. A low whimpering sound. A pool of blood is seen gathering under the huddled right leg of the cell-occupant. This figure is naked, except for a loincloth, and has been bruised on either side of the temples, and bleeds from the surface of the stomach; his right leg is injured. The whimpering stops. Low heart beat, regular. He coughs. It is blood and phlegm. He raises his head cautiously, ducks as if from the bright light, struggles to all fours and crawls to left side of doors. His progress is excruciatingly painful. The heart-rhythms crescendo but never blot out the trundling noise of the crawling. Reaching the wall, he makes an effort and manages to write his initials in his own blood, irregularly and obliquely on the wall. The crescendo of heart-beats stops in the instant of his noisy fall to the ground. The initials A.B. trickle down the wall.

A.B. [*weak, baffled, dispirited*]

Just mine? Just me? . . . . But where are John's . . . And Zak's?

[*He struggles up again and scrawls "Jo" before slipping. The actions repeat till he has finished "Zak" as well. From his fallen position he murmurs*]

A.B. It's only blood. It won't last.

VOICE OVER [*Calm, bureaucratic, of ruthless quietness*]
You frighten me? Hard luck, my friend,
you're not in time, never will be again.
A generation late, that's what you are.
Don't shake your fist at me, young man.
Those fivers are small change to my guns.
I needn't fight you, son, and if I do
it's just to make you feel a little point.
I'll strike you out with one stroke of the pen.
Like this . . . [*Amplified noise of pen scratching*]
A lease upon your life, the freehold gone.
[*This speech seems to start round again like a record but distorts into electronic cacophony at "A generation . . .". Silence prolonged. The figure stirs, coming round. It rises, observes its nakedness and gore. It goes to the door grill and hangs there yelling in a paroxysm that soon softens into irony.*]

A.B. Hey, you bastards, this blood, don't waste it all.
It's blood . . . you know, blood. They say it's good
for potted plants [*Sotto voce*] or planted pot.
[*pause*]
Besides, it's mine, I think, what's left of it . . .
[*He looks down at the blood.*]
Christ, I must leak.
[*He notices the Bible lying on the locker, leans in tired cruciform fashion on the back of the door but relaxes instantly. Picks it up, quoting without opening it*]
And though I give my body to be burned
and have not charity . . . [*Calling out*] Now don't be vague,
give us a Haig . . . poppy; I'll make it grow.
[*Savagely he rips several leaves from the Bible*]

The next best thing to Kleenex, this.
[*He soaks up some of the blood with it as if blotting paper.*]
Leaf to leaf and dust to dust it is.
Make something grow, old rhesus negative.
[*While he is absorbed in doing this, the door is opened quietly and a uniform like a white hospital orderly's is thrown in. There is no underwear and no shoes. A clang shuts the door. Ignoring or ignorant of this, A.B. goes to bars of window hole and drops the bloody pages outside.*]

A.B. Useful stuff, this blood. Blots out the words
and works, you hope, as compost, too.
[*He tries squinting out of the window hole at soil.*]
Ah, now is that a frond of candytuft
or shoot of gloriosa superba. . . .
[*Repeats mopping up operation and returns to window to dispose of it.*]
This blood I sow,
old rhesus negative,
make something grow,
let something live.
[*He turns away and contemplates the huddle of clothing on the floor.*]

A.B. Christ, they didn't leave much of him!
Hey, wake up, now. Come on, wake up.
Poor sod, I must get you to the bed.
[*He gently arranges the uniform as if a body with broken limbs and even more gently begins to raise it in his arms.*]
Light as a feather, must have starved you months.
[*He draws the figure slowly across floor as if a dead-weight person and drapes it leaning against the bed. In course of this the white clothes become stained with his blood.*]
Hold on, old chap, I'll just unzip the bed.
[*Shifts to head of bed finding a bare palliasse only.*]
Huh, soon done. Steady now. That's it, that's it,
gently does it now. You can rest here.
[*To himself*]
Water? Christ, no bloody water. Here,
chew this. It's blood, but only mine. [*He offers him bits of the Bible.*]
[*To himself*]

And full of vitamins if these shakes now
are anything to go on. Hold it, hold it.
No, no, don't touch a drop. I forgot
it's chock a block with truth drugs I should say,
no use at all. And the paper it's printed on's
divine truth. No good at all, useless.
Hey, you wouldn't have a capsule, though.
Poor bugger, where'd you hide a thing like that?

No, don't disturb yourself. I'm all right here . . .
You told 'em nothing naturally, old chap.
Me too. They never got a thing from me.
They'll lay off now a bit. *You* can't take more
and *my* attendant's having tea and toast.
Besides, there's not much more that can be done.
I see you've lost your toenails too. Ah well,
we'll have to cut down on the scissors then.
Roll on demob, death was a washout, eh?
Oh, sorry, wrong war or at least Mark I.
I put one in my ear, cut down their din,
they found it though, capsule, I mean.
And where was yours? What can a man hide
stripped to the buff? A few bloody facts. . . .
I'll let you sleep now, let us sleep now.
No hurry to wake up in the morning, mind.
Goodnight, old chap; no names, no pack-drill, eh?
Of course, if you really wanted to talk, though,
you could tell me anything and everything.
It's quite safe. . . .[*pause*]
Well, yes, you're right, they must have bugged the place.
[*He slumps to the floor in much the position into which he was thrown first. The lights fade down to indicate time passing and fade up again.*]

A.B. [*waking*] Brrr . . . nippy
[*He turns his chest to the bedside and sprawls his hands across the bed, rumpling the legs of the sleeping uniform. He fidgets feet, hunkers and legs seeking a comfortable position which he holds momentarily. He fidgets and stands up, look down.*]

Still there? Not too cold then.
I s'pose they're next for questioning too.
[*He beats his arms and slaps about to warm up. He begins walking round the cell. Dawnlight is coming in at the window.*]
Mmmm, it's not bad, you know, this slight nip
against the skin, mmmm, nice and fresh and clean.
[*He starts around again, three steps, pauses, starts again.*]
Ah yes, I shall, a bit of self indulgence.
I should have walked more often in my shirt,
just in my shirt at dawn or dusk, and felt
the chill nibbling across me, the cold hands
of a cool woman. Yes, and I should 've walked
barechest in the rain, spring rain, downpours,
plainting across me. Too late now, too late.
[*He stops again by the bed and slumps down on the floor, resting his head back against it. Pause. Heavy breathing. He looks down at his chest.*]
A hair. They've left me one of my own hairs.
All is not lost, I'll nurture something there.
[*He blows it, puffs and blows.*]
[*Dispirited*]
No, no, it's not the same. No nip at all.
Not a tingle. But what do you expect
after it's wheezed in and leaked back out
of these flapdoodle lungs? What a [*Coughs*] hope!
[*Beats hands and arms across chest, coughs again partly hamming it*]
How much of the books of Kings remains
[*Spotting Bible on the floor*]
After you make a patchwork suit of them?
Put on the whole armour of God, eh?
For once I'd rather have the Daily Telegraph.
[*He has opened the Bible over his leg like greaves.*]
Not so much warmth in that. Try here. [*The genitals*]
The Second Letter of St. Paul to the French.
Or here. [*The heart*] Now that's more like it I suppose.
That stirs the heart. [*Stage whisper*] Or makes the hackles rise.
[*Dramatic pause*]
My hackles. [*Hammed up search of non-existent pockets*]
They've got my hackles. My hackles, the swine.
[*Pause*]

Dignity. Where's your dignity, man? [*Looks quickly down*]
Still there.
[*Rapidly resumes holy position, Bible on heart*]
I swear to tell the truth, the whole truth
and nothing but the truth, so help me God.
[*Stage whisper*]
Not that they'll get it, though.
[*In sudden anger he hurls the Bible at the door. There is a jangle and rattle as if in response and as if someone is entering but nothing further develops yet. A faint shadow of the window is thrown on the floor by a weakly rising sun. He spots it and edges across to it as if it will shoot away if it observes his approach. A sudden advance and he stamps on the patch of light.*]
Got you, got you.
[*He stamps round the little patch.*]
Take that, and that and that.
Power is a boot stamping on the human face.
[*He squats in the rhomboid of light.*]
Sunbathe! [*He spreadeagles*]
No, no, increases loss of heat.
[*He curls up like a foetus. Stage whisper*]
Ugh, here we go again.
[*He beats the floor with his ankle.*]
Mother, mother,
dear mother, let me in.
[*Impersonates female voice*]
Not tonight, son,
it's daddy's turn.
[*Pause. Sound of heartbeats*][*Sudden frenzy. He leaps up, shouting*]
More sun, more sun, I say.
The dark can't take me.
[*He rushes to the bars of the window as if to reach the sun and thrusts his hands desperately out of the bars. A shadow lunges across the light, there is a thud and he withdraws his arms rapidly, rubbing the wrists. Dispiritedly*]
My bloody bits of Bible in his pipe,
I suppose. They don't take any chances here.
[*Picks Bible up from the door area and flicks through apparently seeking a special page. He rips it carefully out and folds it into a dart. It is smudged with blood from yesterday. After several attempts he manages to fly it high out of the bars. He grips them like a monkey, feet on the wall, and chants.*]

There was a little man
and he had a little gun
and he shot my dart right into the sun, sun, sun.
[*He turns, pauses, reflects, remembers.*]
Quiet, you idiot, you might have woken him.
[*He creeps back to the bed.*]
Good, he is sleeping and the dreams are his.
[*Pauses, reflects*] And I am glad his sleep's so deep and sound.
Still, I have made a promise to myself
of no more dreams. I will remember none.
They cannot make you dream. Nightmare's their game.
They cannot make me dream. I made myself dream.
[*The door jangles as if someone is opening it. A.B. hurries to bars where he leans on elbow, hand to head, pretending to gaze out absorbed. Enter a white-coated medical attendant. He coughs to attract A.B.'s attention. Pause. He coughs again.*]

A.B. [*Without turning*] So far so good. Now say ah!

Med. Sit down.

A.B. [*With exaggerated address sits down precisely where he is.*]

Med. Here. [*He indicates bed. A.B. shakes his head as much as to say "poor fool" to indicate refusal.*]

A.B. Can't budge. My legs have gone.
[*Medical Attendant drags him, limp-legged, over to the bed and slumps him down. He runs like liquid straight back on to the floor in a position identical to that which opens this dawn scene.*]

Med. [*Thumping the bed*] Up!

A.B. —yours. [*He strikes him in the privates and the medico lurches back.*]
Leave him alone, you bastard you.
Can't you see he hasn't had a wink of sleep?

Med. [*Gasping*] You'll have to try a bit better than that.
I know your little game and you're not mad.
There's no one there.

A.B. There is. His name is Tom

Med. And Dick and Harry.

A.B. [*With menace*] His name is Tom, say Tom.

Med. I think you're sane. There's no one there at all.

A.B. I think there is, you know. Take a good look.
[*Medico sheepishly does so.*]

Med. What you might think is no one's business now,
not even yours. There's no one there. See?
[*He thumps the bed again and again is thumped in the privates. This time, provoked, he cuffs A.B.'s head and knocks him over.*]

A.B. [*In process of this*] Leave him alone, you swine.

Med. There's no one there.

A.B. The shadow of a man is there. I know.
And that's more than you are standing there.

Med. A uniform.

A.B. No more and no less than you.

Med. I'll fetch you in a cuddly teddy bear.
What depths of human feeling have we here.
[*Applies stethescope to A.B.'s chest.*]

A.B. [*forgetting situation*]
It's cold. . . . I'm cold all over.

Med. A teddy bear
would keep you warm.

A.B. So long as it arrives
in better shape than Tom, I wouldn't mind.
But you're the deliverer and look at me?

Med. [*Curtly*] Dress.

A.B. [*Rises*] The man himself. Embarrassed, aren't you now?

Med. [*Curtly*] Dress.

A.B. [*Sinking down again, chanting*] Who's afraid of hypothermia now?
What'll they do to you if I up and die?
[*Half rises*] They'll dump you here, flatter than this poor bugger.
[*Stroking Tom*] Who's afraid of hypothermia now?

Med. There are far quicker ways to die than that.
[*He takes out a syringe.*]

A.B. I'm not in any hurry actually. I've plenty of time.
Though I'm sure you are. Another mouth to feed,
the cost of guards, not to mention medicare,
interrogators, torturers and chefs.
I must apologize most awfully
but I'm afraid you'll have to shoot me dead.
I don't die easily.

Med. [*Not really listening, he takes his pulse.*]

A.B. Am I well enough?
To face the firing squad?

Med. You'll be quite fit
When they have finished with you next.

A.B. Oh good.
No sense in wasting bullets on a bag of bones.
So what exactly is your job in here?
You put away your truth-drugs and your prick.
They've tried all that before and failed and failed.

Med. You have no means to tell whether it fails.

A.B. [*Visibly shaken . . . recovering*] I have a means . . . an unshakable means.

[*Pauses for inquiry; none forthcoming*]
I don't know anything you want to know.

Med. We only need to know exactly who you are.

A.B. [*Interrupting*] —That's Tom. You reckon I must be Dick?—

Med. Our records and computers can betray the rest.

A.B. I've no head for figures. My number's up.
[*He makes a V-sign.*]

Med. [*Subtly and suavely*] That's in your jacket.

A.B. [*Rushing to bed and tousling Tom to check on number*]
Liar, liar, liar. [*Waving back of collar in his face*]

Med. So much for human form. That's how we'll break you.
When you're not really looking. You'd like to die.

A.B. [*Recovering*] I've got eyes in my arse for you and all your games.

Med. We'll see, we'll see. We've probably seen to that!
[*Changing to affable tone*]
I'll take these then, [*Indicating clothes*] you're so keen, you say,
on hypothermia. I'll have the heating off
for you. A great help that'll be. What food
would you like us to throw away for you? There's steak,
or roast or game? Any particular breed of dog
you'd like to eat it?

A.B. [*His eyes have never left the clothes.*] He stays with me. Here.

Med. Now, now, don't fall in love with the creatures of time.
[*Mock sympathy, stroking the clothes*] Poor Tom, he's cold, he's cold all over.
[*Mock advice*] We'll break you that way sooner than any other.
[*Mock sympathy*] There, there, you let me have them now. Be good.

We've many other candidates for these
and while you play with them, they die of cold.

A.B. Lend me your syringe. I'll write a charity cheque.

Med. No need for that. But leave them everything
in your will.

A.B. I'll keep my winding sheet, let go.

Med. [*Letting the clothes slip*] I'll help you on with them.

A.B. [*Dashing them from his hand*] No, you will not.

Med. Pick them up.

A.B. [*Gazing at heap*] He's in direst need of care
And medical attention. That's your job.

Med. [*Kicks them at A.B.*]

A.B. Well trained. I see.
[*Medico swings brusquely away, only to return.*]

Med. Just watch me now. You'll see.
[*He squirts syringe to check that it is clear.*]
Enough chat for one day. This won't hurt—much.

A.B. [*Leaping away*] Didn't I say no more of pentathol?

Med. [*Agreeably*] That's right. This little cocktail's not the same.
It's vitamins to keep you going strong.
[*They hover and maneuvre round each other as if in a stiletto fight with a table between them.*]

A.B. [*Panting*] I'll go strong when I'm shit scared which isn't now.

Med. Worse than a kid at the dentist, you are; my God
it's only a little prick.

A.B. And just like you
and all your crowd, you want us all like kids.
But I'm not going to be a good boy and die quiet.

Med. [*pointing syringe upward*] This isn't death, it's life. You're underfed
and prey to any bug that's on the hop.
[*He closes in. A.B. grabs the needle arm and starts to wrest at it.*]

Med. [*extremely patient and calm*] Now don't do that. You haven't got the strength
and I don't need the nourishment.

A.B. Nor me.
I'm going to die of natural causes, see.

Med. You're dying of lost causes but not yet.
I'm not allowed to let you. So stand still.

A.B. You catch me if you can.

Med. If I lunge at you
it could well rip a vein across, or ligament.

A.B. And we're so short of prison hospitals.
Now prison morgues, well, that's another thing.
[*Looks at arms*] Another scab won't notice much, you know.
Especially upon another corpse.

Med. [*Sitting*] Oh well,
You'll soon get tired. It's up to you.

A.B. [*Brightly*] The guards,
why don't you call the guards to hold me down?
They'd enjoy that, unless they're beating someone up.
And what a fool you'd look. So draw your gun.
Oh yes, I see it. Threaten me with death
to make me partial to your euthanasia then.
The will-power never tires.

Med. The body does
and folds the will-power up.

A.B. [*Super-politely*] Mind if I sit?
It takes some time.

Med. Be my guest.

A.B. And what about your other patients, doc?
You got all day to waste?

Med. No, but you have.
So make the most of it.

A.B. [*Suddenly lunging with wad of Bible over syringe needle; it breaks*]
Oh God, our help. . .

Med. [*Furious*]Bugger you.

A.B. But not with that now, eh?
Just enter me as done. And piss off from here.

Med. Oh well, if you must suffer everything
it's up to you.

A.B. [*Not listening, gazing at Bible*] It's blasphemy, you know.
[*The medico exits, a distant human scream is heard.*]
[*A.B. looks at the clothes upon the floor. He observes his shadow; arranges the clothes along his shadow as if dressing it. Stands, shifts to one side to get the shadow properly on to the clothes. Folds hands in front of chest like a vicar praying, then like a Crusader's brass. Kneels and adjusts sleeves to his shadow in this last position. Stands and intones Bible passage from funeral service. He reaches the phrase "in sure and certain hope of the resurrection. . .", stops abruptly and is galvanized into action. He falls almost headlong on to the clothes as if for mouth-to-mouth resuscitation but is in fact searching for the number the medico claimed to be in the collar. Finding it, he crouches up*]

A.B. 10201. . .; 10201. . .ten thousand and more?
Dear old ten thousand two hundred and one.

[*He looks round furtively and then breaking a scab on his leg draws blood. He crawls under the bed, the most inaccessible place, and we hear him muttering as he writes on the wall.*]

A.B. 10201. . .1;0;2;0;1. Tom. . . T;o;m. That's it.
[*As he struggles out from under the bed he knocks his skull on the edge of it. He sits on the floor rubbing his head absent-mindedly.*]

A.B. If they don't want you to get amnesia
What on earth do they knock you on the head for?. . .
Now who am I? They'll never find that out.
It's taken me a devil of a life-time.
So many things that tell me who I am
that cannot make much sense to their machines.
[*He picks up the tattered Bible shut, pretends it is a cassette tape-recorder with an acted irony. He switches it on.*]
Let's pour a slurry in its tiny mind . . .
Now let me see . . .I am the man—Not quite.
I am the man who . . . Not half—Not half enough.
No more of that. I *am* the man . . .Well what?
precisely what? Ah well, I am the *man*,
[*Sheepishly*] the man that cornflakes put in mind of hens.
Or cocks, let's say, it's more ambiguous.
But why and how? I mustn't find that out.
I'm no psychologist. Now don't start that.
If once I found it out they'd cotton on
and that would be a clue of sorts to them . . .
And yet I think I know the reason why.
(There's but to do and die.) My Light Brigade.
Yes, that was it, those soldiers I once had
when I was little, like the Duke of York
but not ten thousand men, only a few.
The war, it was. That's right, the Second War.
My regiment of guards, and man for man
impossible to replace. I broke enough.
Dunkirk, there was to play, and Normandy.
Matchsticks could mend a few, but only heads.
—If only they still could with the blockheads here.—
The casualties would look much realer then.

None of your modern plastic rubbish, that.
But only tread on one and curtains it was.
[*Looks down at Bible*]
Bugger, it's run out of tape. Maybe it's wise.
Bright as silver their insides were, you know,
like crinkled silver paper but glossy still.
Curve of a torso a torque of concave forms,
the mirror convexity from tail to wing
of chicken that we kept and silver white
in the sun, squawking fragmentary smithereens.
That section much the same as cornflake warp.
[*Pause. Ponderously dramatic*]
Not until now the connexion with Smith's crisps.
It's difficult to make this very clear.
They'll never follow anything of this.
[*Pause*]
Enough nostalgia. Let me be the man
who found a flywheel governing his head
and classified ten types of human fart.
[*His eye falls on a bit of Bible still on the floor. He marks it*]
10201: Tom. [*Looks round as if suddenly lost*]
Where the hell is this?
[*He folds another dart out of it and launches it through the bars. As he turns from the bars he catches sight of their shadow on the ground. He stops beside them so that looking down he sees them more or less horizontal. He regards them as steps. He puts his hands forward as if about to dive from a diving board. He climbs up them like this. At the top, he turns and rushes down, pretending to stumble.*]

A.B. [*Wryly*] No, I'm no longer in the swim. Try this.
[*He puts his hands up and pretends to roll down his collar, then he places his hands behind his back as if tied up, closes his eyes and fumbles his way up the steps. Head bowed, he pauses dramatically at the top and in a voice parodying the melodramatic, he quotes*]

A.B. "O World, O Life, O Time!
On whose last steps I climb. . ."
[*Own voice*]
Enough of that. Try something else:

"Pray put aside my beard, that hath done no harm."
[*Strokes clean-shaven (well, three day's growth) chin, reflectively*]
No, that's not on. . .
[*Pause for thought*]
"It is a far better thing. . .
[*Vehement*] Not bloody likely!

[*He raises his head high with an assumed hauteur and then he kneels as if to the block. He voices a swishing sound and instantly lurches himself sideways off the steps. He lies doggo for a few seconds, then springs to his feet. He feels for a halo round his head and then for a tail behind him.*]
Christ, is this hell? Or high water?
The only rising I will see?
[*He moves over and for the first time yet he sits upon the edge of the bed. Pause. Looking toward the head of the bed and as if addressing someone, he says.*]

A.B. Good morning, father. I won't say
it's good to see you.
[*Rapidly he shifts up to the position where the father would be and replies to himself. This rapid change of "person" happens with each change of "speaker" in the following exchanges.*]

A.B. as PRIEST. Good morning, my son.
These few precious moments alone with you
are all that they will grant to me, alas.
So let us use them wisely for your soul's good.
You wait immediately upon the life to come.

A.B. Say that again; it's life without remission.

A.B. as P. My son, is this a time to joke and play?
Eternity lies before you, eternal fire
or everlasting bliss. Is your soul right now?

A.B. It's all right with me.

A.B. as P. I don't know what to say
To make you serious.

A.B.   You're serious enough,
father, if they sling you into one of these.
These scabs and bruises, look, are serious.

A.B. as P. My son, they're less than nothing in the light
of everlasting truth, in the eyes of God.

A.B. Well, thanks for that small comfort, father.
This cell's not serious, either, in the church's eyes
so what are you here for? You could be praying.
But I know why you're here. You'll stand and watch
while any thug gets on with death and torture
if there's the chance to catch a passing soul.
Well, this soul isn't passing, not your way at least;
it's past; long past the point of heaven and hell.
[*Rising*] Here I stand, and I can do no other now. . .
But if I could I would and not with words
and not with dignity and holy calm.
[*He subsides, sheepish.*]

A.B. as P. The Church's strength is not as men see it,
But spiritual. The will of God confronts
the power of men in ways you cannot see.

A.B. No, nor feel, either, and nor do they.

A.B. as P. Have faith, my son, and do not fear the ways
of men that kill the body only. They want
your soul and that the grace of God forbids.

A.B. There's nothing else they haven't had off me.
You wouldn't carry on you a spare set of nails?
[*Pause*]
Only the five? You'd better keep them then.
Your only chance of the stigmata, I should think.

A.B. as P. My son, vent all your anger on my head.
I do not mind and you are not to blame.
Many's the man who has done much the same
in your shoes. You stand in such a dread,

hysteria comes too easily to a fellow.
So many times I've had to minister
to men in your condition that I know
a kinder calm will come upon you soon.
And when it does the Church is here to listen.

A.B. From where I sit it looks as if the Church,
yourself included, bends to the power of men.
Or else why are you here?

A.B. as P. My duty, son.

A.B. Your duty to the state, more like, than me.
They summoned you and you came running here,
a sadist to an accident.
Shall I confess?
What have they asked you to confess me of?

A.B. as P. What passes now between your lips to me
is secret as confession, only God
shall hear whatever it is you want to say.

A.B. And if they put you to the torture, too?

A.B. as P. My priestly office and my sworn vows
would keep your words intact.

A.B. How right you are
since I shall tell you nothing.

A.B. as P. Will you kneel,
receive the sacrament?

A.B. I will not kneel.

A.B. as P. [*Stage whisper*] Is there a message I can smuggle out?

A.B. [*As if betraying whisper*] Yes. Tell God not to expect me . . . ever.
[*He stands, stretches*] Well, nothing there a bug can bugger about.
[*From outside in the yard comes the sound of marching feet. An order is barked and a volley is heard. A.B. rushes to the window.*]

A.B. [*Shouting*] Bastards, bastards!
[*A guard knocks his hands brutally off the bars again and thrusts the rifle-butt at him to keep him away from the window. A.B. grabs the thick end of the butt yet struggles pointlessly as his hands are relentlessly pulled against the bars and repeatedly knocked on them.*]

A.B. [*Dejected, leaning close in to left of the bars, sucking his knuckles*]
Well, that one had no mask. What's left of a language?
[*He glimpses again the shadow of the bars upon the wall now. He sprawls beside it and then pretends to play upon a harp. He mouths the twanging and plonking to a lugubrious rhythmless plain chant to the point where the audience would be driven to exclaim, "Stop!"*]

A.B. I might as well get some early practice in.
"And flights of angels sing thee to thy rest."
Poor maskless comrade, nameless and afraid.
[*He stops with a gesture of disgust.*]
The rest is silence, friend.
[*He doodles with his hands shadowing on the wall. Eventually, he shapes a shadow wolf or some predator and gets it behind the shadow bars.*]
Rodents the only race alongside man
That have increased their hold on earth with him.
Poor wolf, they've turned you, too, into a dog.
[*He gets up and comes to sit again on the edge of the bed.*]

A.B. Now, bring the edges of the tongue to meet
above the centre, thus you make a tube.
(And not what you are thinking, either, lad.)
Next draw the tip of the tongue inside the tube
and up and back into the roof of the mouth.
Now gently move the tongue so slightly back
and forth and up and down: the flywheel in the head
and not what you were thinking, lad. Odd.
Is this a lingual illusion or Freudian tip?
[*Puzzled*]
How is it done? How long go on before
the mouth gets sore? What distances are covered?
and would I get proper medical care?
[*This whole speech has been rendered haltingly as A.B. follows his own instructions.*]

[*The doors jangle and clang. Enter a real priest of a vaguely Orthodox/ Catholic persuasion. The opening of the conversation is rendered somewhat comic for the audience and baffling for the priest because A.B. is constantly experimenting with the flywheel in his head.*]

A.B. [*Hamming absorption, making no effort to recognize entry of priest*]

Priest. [*Coughs*]

A.B. Amen.

Priest. My son, I have a difficult task to perform.

A.B. [*Flywheeling first*]
Uh, so have I. Now would you like a go?

Priest. My son, it's hard enough, don't make it harder.

A.B. [*Snapping out of it with cold fury*]
Not half as hard as mine. What do you want?
Sympathy?

Priest. My son, it's sympathy
that brings me here awhile to speak with you.
We know the way you feel.

A.B. That's good to hear
but if it's true why are you standing there?

Priest. They asked me did I want a word with you
before you die. (There now my task is done
and not how I'd have wished it done to you)
How could a priest refuse his priestly work?

A.B. [*With some shock*] Me die? [*Pause; with anger*] I get it now. They lack the nerve,
the bastards with the guns, they lack the nerve
to tell me so themselves. A point to me.
[*Furious*] And so they send for you and you agree to do
their dirty work.

Priest. It's better from a priest.

A.B. And you'd collaborate with murderers?

Priest. My son, I had to come in any case
to hear your last confession on this earth.

A.B. [*thinking aloud, cold, analytic*] If their belief is strong enough to date
to send you here and do the holy thing
then you should never have complied with them.
What other power has the Church than that?
Who else has any power to counter them?
You might have made one flunkey think again
but chatting here does nothing.

Priest. The Church's strength is never seen by men—

A.B. [*Interjecting*]
Too bloody true.

Priest. I come to set your soul at ease, my son.
A duty not contained by earthly time.
Forget the quarrels of the day. Think God.
The Church can take no sides in fleshly wars.
God's servants are the same to all mankind.

A.B. Like fog, you mean?

Priest. You understand my words
although this time of need hardens your heart.
Your heart you've had to harden in these trials;
the Church is not so blind to human frailty
as sometimes seems the case. She has an eye
for human error sharper than idealists like you,
an ear for human misery like yours. Her touch
is gentler than a lover's on a wound.
She knows all human weakness; it is hers,
her history a record of the worst.
Come to the window, look out in the yard
and trust my ways a little more, my son.

Good men I've helped, and bad, brave and fearful,
to do what you must do this dusk.

A.B. [*Incredulous*] The bars? Those bars?
D'you think I've been so little time in here
I've never looked beyond the bars before?
How long, d'you think, a man would be in here
before he took a gasper at those bloody bars?

Priest. You haven't looked out there before this moment
knowing the hour you must die. This dusk.
Come now, my son, and count the paces there
and fix your bearings. Look, underfoot
it's shingle. You wouldn't want to stumble on that.

A.B. I will not comply.

Priest. I wish you would. You ought to die a man.
Courage must be prepared if your cause is just.

A.B. A coward's death embarrasses the living.
It may be that's the last laugh I shall have.

Priest. [*Turning from the bars*] Well . . . I suppose the sight is little use
under the blindfold you'll have on, tonight.

A.B. [*With cold fury which baffles the priest*]
I will not wear a blindfold, nor will I walk
that way—nor any way a priest would guide.
I shall not die out there.

Priest. Prepare yourself.
You may take on the power of man so far
as you have done but no further as you see.
They have you in their power now to die.
Nothing can stop them here. No force survives
to mount last minute rescues of a man.
Only the power of God and your own mind
can save you from an ignominious death.
Who knows what spark of doubt a noble end
might fire in someone's mind?

A.B. You come too.
Now that might cause a stir. But no, not you,
you've still your priestly tasks to do on earth.
The blunt refusal of a priest to play
charades with murderers might still have raised
an eyebrow or two. Or possibly a spark.
But I'll not die out there.

Priest [*Needled*] Such touching faith
in human agency. I haven't seen the like
since Hollywood was going great guns.
So why not spare some faith for God, not man.
He is your stay. He is our only stay
in troubled times.

A.B. Then let him stay the execution.

Priest. In his will lies your peace. Men's deeds
he turns to his account in time, my son,
if not in time then in eternity.
You must believe your death is in his will.

A.B. Oh sure, I'll leave my will behind, shall I?
Here, you shall have my library [*Proffers tattered Bible*]
I'm sure a death within the will of God
will feel so much less painful than my own.

Priest. There's a special providence in the fall of a sparrow.

A.B. Make that the fall of the system, I'm your man.
[*Pause*] And of a Church that silently condones the state.
[*Pause*] Goodbye.
Father, I said goodbye to you.

Priest. You see. You have as prisoner no power
to make me leave your presence. I stand here
and I can do no other. I have brought you
the sacrament, the offer of God's mercy.
Think what it is you say before I leave you.
This tired and wizen face, this perished body

and, yes, this narrow mind, if you insist,
is the last friend, the last human features
you will see before you see the face of God.
Think long, my son, before you send me out
through that door.

A.B. Think long yourself before you send
a man through that door, [*With fury*] before you show the steps
it takes to reach the stake, collaborator.
Goodbye.
Priest. [*Surreptitiously leaving some Bible scraps on the locker*]
Very well, my son, your last free action,
your last act upon this earth is to send
God's mercy through that door.

A.B. [*vehement*] That door
leads to the guards, the torturers and thugs.
God comes in at the window. [*Indicating the sunlight*]
And take your tracts.
There's little time for reading left to me.
My God, they're mine. I folded them.
You bloody idiot, can't you see a thing?
[*Indicates bloody writing on the Bible pages, furious*]

Priest. It cannot be this way. If guards found this
the priest would never be allowed again
inside these walls to visit dying souls
and all the bibles would be confiscated.

A.B. [*Almost dumbstruck with fury*] You bloody idiot, look, can't you read
or do you leave that for the Pope to do?

Priest. Lucky for you I found it, not the guards.

A.B. There's a man's name here, written in blood.
Probably all that's left of him, poor bugger,
and that's too much for these thugs and for you
by the looks of it. All that's left of a man,
one of their victims, the only witness this is
and the name's probably wrong even then.

Can't you get that into your thick head at all?
[*Pleading*] Lodge it in your mind. Let it come back to you
at odd moments and trouble your peace of mind.
This is the name of your conscience from today on.

Priest. You men of action, you have to play the game
right to the last possible moment. This is nothing,
a false consolation, and you know it too.
I've saved you from another hour of torture—

A.B. [*interjecting*] And bring us not to the ordeal for thine is the power. . .
[*Musing*] I didn't even know the poor bastard.
I wonder what he told them, how he died,
what was he up against, whether the priest came.

Priest. [*Sotto voce; proffering rear flyleaf of pocket bible and a pencil and backing to cover spy-hole in door*] I'll take a message out. Who's it for?

A. B. [*Dejected*] Oh, never mind . . . No, wait a minute, though.
Tell every one from now on that you confess
there died a man, today, in this prison,
who said that cornflakes via soldiers are cocks
and add 10201 Tom. It may be right.

Priest. [*Serious*] A code?

A.B. A code of honour, don't you think?

Priest. [*Jotting*] Suppose your man may never approach me?

A.B. [*laughing*] You wouldn't know whether he does or not.
D'you want to be an accomplice? Come off it, father.

Priest. And is there some last thing to send you in?

A.B. A submachine-gun wouldn't come amiss. [*Wryly regarding Bible*]
A Shakespeare would be something.

Priest. [*Following his eye*] A lesser book.
God bless you, my son, my prayers go with you now.

A.B. And are they bullet-proof?

[*Priest bows out.*] Goodbye.

A.B. Well, that made his day.
[*A.B. sits upon the edge of the bed. Prolonged silence*]

A.B. [*cheerily*] Now let me see. My last great work on earth
and all the afternoon to get it done.
Just the odd shot or two out in the yard
to shake one's concentration. Ideal conditions.
Now what's it to be—or possibly not to be?
I could complete my classification of farts;
I've all the raw materials ready here;
or ride the flywheel seven further miles.
[*Desperate*] Christ! Nothing but a few sticks of shadow
to pass the time. They've shifted a foot already.
I could dub in the sound: tick-tock, tick-tock, tick-tock.
[*He approaches the shadows and laboriously counts.*]
One, two, three, four, five.
My, what a time that took. A stave, a stave.
I'll write my funeral music right up the wall.
I'll outstravinsky him. Why then, why there, why thus. . .
Now how does a clef go?
[*He makes several passes and gestures over the shadows but does not seem to get the hang of it.*]
Too late to make it now.
You're on your own, Pierre Boulez.
[*He wanders back to the bed and sits, head in hands.*]
No, no. That's not the way, dear oh dear no.
[*He strikes the pose of The Thinker.*]
That's much more in keeping with our life and times.
A better sense of occasion.
[*Returns to normal position*]
Nothing on telly.
[*Gets up and pretends to twiddle knobs under the shadows*]
This government makes me sick. There's interference
even on television. And you can't turn it off.
[*Pause*] A drowning man sees all his previous life.
Let's try that now. Lay back, let yourself go.

[*He sprawls back on the bed, resting his head on his hands upon the pillow. Suddenly he raises head from the neck up, and strains to look round.*]
No trick-cyclists hanging about? Right to begin. . .
[*Prolonged silence*]

[*Pensive*] No, I don't want it all. I think the time
has come to exercise some censorship. . .
[*Musing*] Ahhhhh . . . yes. [*Pause.*] Ummmmmmm . . . good.
[*Pause*] Ouch! [*He half-rises and subsides.*] No more of that. [*Pause.*]
. . .That bird, the one in the duffel. It had a hood—
down—and that spiral of the most auburn hair.
A tartan-lining, two triangles just showing
each side of her throat, the head turned,
the rod of muscle thrusting to the ear.
A distant look in her eyes. She never saw me.
That's right. Standing in the arch of a shop door.
I know the name of the shop to this day.
But my girl, I don't even know your name.
[*Pause*] Now, why should I remember you today?
[*He swings his feet rapidly to the floor and sits on edge of bed like a psychiatrist.*]

Psych. This is obviously a suppressed image of innocence
verging on knowledge. What else do you recall?

A.B. [*Swinging furiously back to prone position*]
Innocence be damned! An advert for a coat.
[*He leaps up and goes to the bars.*]
For pity's sake, can't you provide better than this?
[*Wildly indicating shadow while looking up and out of window*]
The shadow of a tree, a silhouette of shade?
And keep far hence the shadow of the dog?
[*Momentary clouding of sun*]
That's right! Typical. Go on take offence
but this time remember I'm coming after you.
Bloody pantheon, think they own the place.
I'll cast a spell on them if it's the last thing I do.
[*Prancing round in a circle*]
Rain, rain, go away.
Come again another day,
Come again on mother's washing day.

[*Unnoticeably during the next few moments the sun does return. A.B. returns to sit on the edge of the bed.*]

A.B. [*Musing*] I shall call her Jeannette, no surname, though. . .
It's wrong. The whole damn system wrong from the start.
It's not your auburn hair I'm after, nor your face.
I never even saw it. But now I seem to see
one leg was raised, the sole flat on the façade,
marble that was, the cone of worsted skirt
solid it seemed, the rust red of bracken,
over the other leg. No sex in that.
A symphony in red. A cubist sketch.
So why should I remember you at all. . .
I used to like the bracken about August time.
Higher than my head but losing strength,
great billows of green that seemed deflating.
I liked that. No politics, either, there
though of course it did turn somewhat red.
[*Shouting as if to a deaf mute*] Hey, Freud, I said no politics in that.
Is that okay? Oh busy dreaming, are you?
Wish I had the time. Sorry I spoke. . .
Plaiting of rainwater along the kerb,
the noise of drops flicking and ticking the leaves.
[*Abrupt heckling*] Snap out of this, you bastard, where's the people?
You don't seem to enjoy them half as much. . .
[*Prolonged pause*]
[*Musing*] What I enjoy is the lone athlete out front—
he's got some things to run from nowadays;
the violinist going strong at eighty-one,
what's his name? lively as a gardener still;
the carver of stone hacking away on a gun-step;
the bored scientist in the lone night watch—
the blokes who make it all depend on them.
And I never met them once. I knew them though.
Right here [*Pats head*] I know them all right here.
[*Points out brain with finger*]
That's where the bullet goes.
[*Licks finger and marks an X there*] X marks the spot.
[*Pause; blaspheming*]
And can you be baptized with the baptism wherewith I am baptized?

[*Musing*] Of course, if all of them are six foot guards
I'll have to stand on tiptoe, I should think.
[*He practises, stumbles.*]
Damn.
[*He goes back to sit on the bed.*]
[*Tenderly*] Jeannette, [*Calling*] Jeannette, I shall call you my Jeannette.
And if the mind has any drag in this world
something will come into your head today
for you are all I have to think on now,
[*He strokes tenderly the outline of his shadow head on the wall.*]
and, sadly, young enough you are to me
to be a daughter when I really need a wife
for what I want to feel before I die
is love and you are all there is, Jeannette,
for me to try it on. I suppose you know.
Someone must have married you long since.
Your hair, that spiral swathe, I'd like to touch it.
My touch would loiter near your breast, between.
[*Impatient*] No, that's not memory, that's me today.
I must be sex-starved, your duffel gave no clue
though all that auburn hair would lead that far.
[*Calmer*] There's nothing much I want of you, Jeannette.
Fat chance there is of troubling you, my girl,
and yet I'd like to know whatever it was
you were attending to that night of beginning dark.
But then I can't remember what it was
I must have been about. So that is that.
Jeannette, I wish you health and happiness,
a handy man and children too if you want them
and something you might occasionally call love
and sometimes sit with him odd evenings quiet
and what you do after that's your own business.
The body may be good to you, my dear.
The mind is hell without the body's love.
I need a rose to wear to honour you,
sweet memory of all that could not be.
I'm sorry it must be a rose of blood.
But do not think I linger here for you,
don't think I'm dying for the love of you
or likes of you. The things that come unsought:
the dragonfly between skyscraping blocks;

brown tinge of a leaf on the pavement a week,
now ochre, now washed away in a night's rain;
a good pint of beer with unexpected friends.
These will turn up despite regimes, Jeannette,
and people mostly snatch them on the hop.
That's what you did in the shop door surely.
[*He gets up and goes to lean his back on the doors. He raises one leg, placing his sole on the door at about knee height and endeavours from there to stare out through the bars.*] I bet you watched the moon, driftmeal of clouds.
That powder-compact lid on a shawl of cloud.
Your face. No, no, I didn't see the moon.
To tell the truth on many nights like that
awaiting action I used to notice her
and that's the way she mostly seemed those nights
after hot sun and heavy evening showers
a threat of big rain-drops still in the air,
clouds tinged with salmon pink of sunken sunset.
[*Moves to window*]
That's how I find the moon for you that night.
I used to like it too when there was mist,
its aurora of blue and iridescent haze
around the full. [*Looking out*]
Goodbye, moon, goodbye.
You always were too bland for me, I think,
not rough enough around the edges, either.
[*Returns to the bed*]
[*Absently outlining shadow head with stroking hand*]
What did you see, Jeannette, in the bland old moon?
A crystal ball with all your future told?
Did Mr. Right turn up that very night?
How has it gone, your life, I mean, not mine.
How many cons have you exploded now?
Was love what they made out to you when young?
Is there much left of it now to last a bit?
Ever get a snifter at freedom, lass, and take to it?
Jeannette, tell me, tell me honestly now,
what better than a cup of tea when tired?
[*He goes to the grill and shouts.*]
What better than a cup of tea when dying?
[*Returning, muttering*]
They wouldn't have the decency to poison it.

[*Urgent, pleading*]
Now, listen hard, Jeannette, I'm saying this
only because you cannot hear a word,
if any of this comes through read and destroy.
It won't be needed on this earth again.
I have a certain marvellous thing to tell.
[*Confidentially*] I hope they never ask for my last request.
I'd like the sun a little warmer please,
the mind a little quieter than sleep,
a ruthless firing-squad with deadly aim
but most of all the certain guarantee
of sure oblivion, god-proof, waterproof.
Not psychic are you, I hope, Jeannette?
but just my crazy luck if you say you are.
Over and out. That won't get through at all.
Old Rhine, expending hours and hours to send
circles, squares and triangles mind to mind,
and no great shakes at that, either, it seems.
Try anything once.
[*He gets up and standing on one leg describes a circle with the other.*]
Now concentrate. Hard.
[*Like a stork, eyes closed*]
Again. And weave a circle round him thrice
for he on money due hath fed and sunk the bulk
of Paradise. . .
[*On the third spin he stumbles and falls in a heap.*]
Bastard.
[*He beats the ground.*] Bastard. Bastard.
[*Getting up*] Well, I suppose he was, the poor bugger,
but he had two thieves for company at least.
[*There is a jangle of keys; both the doors are flung open and eventually two soldiers armed with hip revolvers and truncheons swinging from the belt enter. A priest attempts to follow them in.*
As soon as he hears the door-noises, A.B. goes rapidly across to the window where he grasps the outside bars in his fists raised above his head. The guards find him thus and go each side of him, expecting to have to drag him from them.]

A.B. [*Furious, determined*] If that priest comes in I will not budge from here.

1st Guard. Now don't be difficult, mate, we might get rough.

A.B. If he comes in you'll have to break my arms.

2nd Guard. [*Conciliating*] He's got his work to do the same as us.

A.B. This show's on me and I won't have him here.

1st Guard. He doesn't want you, father, wait outside.
[*To A.B.*] Now come along my lad. Let go those bars.
[*He is surprised when A.B. does so without more argument. He releases his hands and looks at them as if foreign objects, at a loss. Then brightly*]

A.B. [*One step forward*] I haven't any pockets in this rig.
Mind if I borrow yours? [*He puts out a hand to each of them. They edge back, hands to holsters.*]

1st Guard. Hold hard, there ain't no hurry. Sit on the bed.

2nd Guard. That's right, mate, take the weight off your feet.

A.B. That job was yours I thought. [*But he does so*]
[*The first guard approaches with a blindfold. A.B. shifts back against the wall.*]

1st Guard. Lean forward, mate, let's get this on.

A.B. [*Shakes head*] I will not wear a mask.

1st Guard. That's up to you.
It wouldn't bother me whichever you do,
But we've had further orders now and all
the convicts have to wear a mask.

A.B. My God,
they frightened someone might reveal some secret
to God? You needn't put it on just yet.
I like to know the way I walk. D'you mind?

2nd Guard. So long as you agree, you know, to wear
the thing as soon as we reach the yard door.
Here, put this jacket on. It's cold out there.
Surprising how cold it gets these summer nights.
Oh, and you'll want something on your feet.
That shingle's something terrible, you know.
[*He ducks his head out the door. The priest immediately reappears.*]
Not you. Hoy, shoes, in twenty one and quick.

1st Guard. He thinks he's sensitive. You think he is?
Well so am I, although it don't appear.
My method is to get it done. Sharp's the word.
And when it's done, it's done. The doing hurts,
that's what I say, so get it over and done
and when it's done, finished. Him, he never forgets.
[*The priest's hand pokes round the door with shoes.*]

2nd Guard. Now here we are. I help you on with them. [*He kneels.*]
Bit stiff, I shouldn't wonder, eh? Not bad. [*He stands.*]

1st Guard. Hands behind your back now, mate, I got
to tie this rope.

A.B. I thought we had agreed
these things could wait until we reached the door.

2nd Guard. Well, not the rope, see, we have to watch it now.
Some rules is rules and others we can bend.

A.B. Now look. If you insist on rope, okay.
But you'll have to knock me out to get it on.
I said I'd let you do your little rites
the moment that we reach the door.

2nd Guard. Ah, well. . .
I don't know if we can. Now what d'you think?

1st Guard. Here, it'll be all right. You take the rope
and if he struggles then I'll knock him out.
[*As the second guard fumbles to catch and tidy the rope, A.B. lunges forward and grasps him in a stranglehold. Both are utterly surprised. He gets a good grip, possibly with the rope before the first guard comes into action. A fierce struggle ensues. The first guard draws his truncheon but there's little room to maneuvre and the second guard becomes A.B.'s shield.*]

A.B. [*Taunting*] Useless, useless, you'll have to use your gun.

1st Guard. Father! Ouf, you bastard. [*He draws*]
[*A.B. succeeds in killing the second guard. He is shot dead himself at close range. As he dies, he cries out*]

A.B. Jeannette!
[*The first guard quickly kicks him off the second, takes a cursory heart-count and runs out.*]

1st Guard. Doctor, doctor, fetch a doctor, quick.
[*Enter the priest. He looks both corpses over, cursorily, using a foot, turns and exit. Enter a white-coated medico, a stethescope hanging from his pocket. He turns them over without stooping, like the priest. As he is about to go, he turns and gives A.B. an extra, bloody-minded kick. Re-enter the first guard, shocked and non-plussed. He stands in a daze, glances round.*]

1st Guard. What did he say? Now what on earth was it?
Jeannette, that's it. Quick.
[*He fumbles in his pockets and finds a stub of pencil. He searches about and finds the battered and bloody copy of the Bible. He snatches a bit out and very laboriously writes "Jeannette."*]

1st Guard. One n and two t's, that's it. Something at least.
[*A final glance round, a shrug*]
Why him and not me?
[*As he shuts the cell doors the lights fade instantly.*]

CURTAIN.